Meni Caroutas is the host of *The Missing Australia* podcast, which has garnered almost 3 million downloads and consistently ranks at the top of the True Crime charts.

After working as a policeman in Kings Cross in the 1980s, Meni turned to journalism and has since worked on Channel Ten's *Hard Copy* and Channel Nine's *Missing Person's Unit* and *A Current Affair*, and Channel Seven's *Today Tonight*, and as a producer on Channel Seven's *Border Security*. He has been interviewed for books (including Justine Ford's *Unsolved Australia*), websites (such as Kidspot) and true crime podcasts (Mamamia's *True Crime Conversations*, Gary Jubelin's *I Catch Killers* and many more).

SOMEONE SOMEWHERE KNOWS SOMETHING

SOMEONE SOMEWHERE KNOWS SOMETHING

MENI CAROUTAS

HarperCollinsPublishers

HarperCollins*Publishers*
Australia • Brazil • Canada • France • Germany • Holland • India
Italy • Japan • Mexico • New Zealand • Poland • Spain • Sweden
Switzerland • United Kingdom • United States of America

HarperCollins acknowledges the Traditional Custodians of the lands upon which we live and work, and pays respect to Elders past and present.

First published on Gadigal Country in Australia in 2025
by HarperCollins*Publishers* Australia Pty Limited
ABN 36 009 913 517
harpercollins.com.au

HarperCollins*Publishers*
Macken House, 39/40 Mayor Street Upper
Dublin 1, D01 C9W8, Ireland

A catalogue record for this book is available from the National Library of Australia

ISBN 978 1 4607 6754 2 (paperback)
ISBN 978 1 4607 1851 3 (ebook)
ISBN 978 1 4607 3332 5 (audiobook)

Cover design by Hazel Lam, HarperCollins Design Studio
Cover image by Daryl Scott Walker / Stills.com
Photographs courtesy of the subject's family, unless otherwise specified
Author photograph by NewsCorp
Typeset in Bembo Std by Kirby Jones

Printed and bound in the United States

For all those who never came home – the missing whose names fade from headlines but never from the hearts of those who love them. This book is for you, and for your families who search in silence, who refuse to give up, who carry hope through heartbreak. May your stories be heard and may the truth one day find its way home.

To my wife, Susie: your unwavering belief in me has been my anchor. And to my children, Bella, Tim, Ben and Tia: your love reminds me every day why this work matters, and inspires me to never give up.

Contents

Foreword

by Bruce Morcombe OAM

Have you ever lost your breath when, for an instant, you could not see your child? It could have been at the shops, or when you realised they were late from school or sport or visiting a friend.

Relive that panic.

Where could they be?

You feel as though you've been struck by lightning. For some, the flash lasts longer, you cannot breathe.

Where the hell are they?

Gone!

Never to be seen again.

When a person goes missing, no matter what their age, it causes immense suffering for those left wondering. They will be forever tortured by unresolved loss. Far too many ordinary people spend the rest of their lifetime with unanswered questions.

For almost eight years I walked that walk. So too did my wife, Denise, and our two remaining sons, Dean and Bradley. The last time we saw our 13-year-old son and brother, Daniel James Morcombe, was on 7 December 2003.

For almost eight years the search for Daniel would be the largest missing person case in Australia.

We did eventually get answers. As sad as they were, at least we knew. Daniel's remains were retrieved from bushland during August and September 2011. He was finally laid to rest on 7 December 2012.

Not long after Daniel went missing, we met Meni Caroutas. He interviewed us for a TV program he was working on. Over the course of 20 years, I have come to respect Meni because he has remained a true fighter for the missing. He is passionate about finding the answers and being a voice for those who do not wish to or can no longer speak.

Over that time, Meni and I have shared stories and worked on projects together in an attempt to generate public interest in a subject often not discussed. With advances in technology and forensic science, and the advent of social media, new light can be shone on the dark world of those who have been left devastated by the sudden disappearance of a family member, loved one, friend, work colleague, school mate or neighbour.

We call that hope.

Don't give up on the missing. Please!

Bruce Morcombe OAM

Preface

As a young boy, I was always going to be a journalist or a cop. I had an insatiable curiosity and a hunger for news. I started reading the daily paper back in the 1970s when I was about eight, simply because it was for sale in the milk bar my family owned.

It was the crime stories that captivated me. The dreadful acts people committed against each other horrified me, but I was also fascinated by the heroes who locked up the criminals and made the streets safer. Reporters and detectives quickly became my idols. They were the ones chasing truth and justice, and I knew that was what I wanted to do with my life.

After high school, I applied for countless cadetships with newspapers, but nothing came of them. So I went to university to study History and English Literature. Then, a year later, an offer came from the NSW Police Force. It felt like the right path.

While at the police academy, I requested to be stationed at Darlinghurst Police Station in Sydney, one of the busiest in the state. I wanted to be in the thick of it, to learn fast and hard.

In October 1984, I graduated and began my police career. Within a year, I was transferred to Kings Cross, where the streets were a wild mix of carnival, circus and crime. It wasn't long before I rose through the ranks and joined the detectives. It was the notorious 1980s, and both Darlinghurst and Kings Cross police would later face the spotlight of the Wood Royal Commission into police corruption.

In 1989, crooked cops set me up with false allegations. After I was cleared, I demanded an investigation into what had happened to me, but the NSW Police Force swept it under the carpet, and those responsible were allowed to leave the force without facing any consequences. So I made the difficult decision to go public about corruption within the police internal security unit.

That decision changed everything. After my appearance on the ABC's *7.30 Report*, a television executive offered me a job as a reporter on a new tabloid current affairs show called *Hard Copy.* I didn't want to leave the NSW Police, but my complaints had been ignored and I knew I had to make a choice. The system wasn't going to change from within.

So, in 1991, I left the job I loved and became a journalist – embarking on my other dream career. Early on, I began covering stories about missing people. As a cop, I had dealt with countless cases of runaway kids who'd ended up in Kings Cross, drawn by the bright lights and excitement. Too many of them never made it out alive. The first missing person case I reported on as a journalist was that of 16-year-old Debbie Ashby, who vanished in 1987.

Even though I had switched careers, my commitment to truth and justice never wavered. I knew that through journalism, I could still make a difference. By shining a light on unsolved cases, I could help families find their missing loved ones. That belief is still what drives me.

Today, there are 2600 long-term missing persons in Australia – that is, people who have been missing for more than three months. Each missing person leaves behind a ripple of heartache. For every person who disappears, it's estimated that 12 others are affected. That's over 30,000 people living with the pain of not knowing where their loved one is or what happened to them. It's a silent crisis for too many families.

Of course, not every person reported as missing wants their whereabouts known. Unless they're a child, the missing person's privacy must be respected. In such cases, the police will tell the family that the missing person is alive and safe but doesn't want to be contacted.

Many of the families whose loved ones are missing have told me that it's the not knowing that's the worst. Riding that emotional rollercoaster is a nightmare they can't wake up from. And until they know what happened to their loved one, they can't truly move forward.

That's why I do what I do. The truth matters. These families deserve answers.

When all the leads dry up, cases go cold, but they're never closed. All it takes is new evidence, a fresh lead or a piece of information from the public to reignite an investigation. That's why I started *The Missing Australia* podcast. I wanted to reach out, to give these cases the attention they deserve, and to urge anyone with information to come forward. I believe, deep down, that *someone, somewhere, knows something.*

And many of them have heard my call. People have come forward. Thanks to those brave individuals, we've seen significant breakthroughs in a number of cases.

This book is about those cases and others, about the families who refuse to give up hope, and about the people who finally decided to speak up.

If you've listened to my podcast, you already know the power of community in solving these cases. And if you're holding this book, maybe you're the one who has the missing piece of the puzzle. If you know something, I hope that reading these stories will inspire you to come forward. Because your information could change everything.

These families need answers. And together, we can help them find the truth.

Debbie Ashby

1

An Indelible Mark

Debbie Ashby

Australia is a vast wild land, but its vastness hides a chilling truth: more than 2600 souls have vanished into its shadows, becoming part of a grim statistic. These are the long-term missing, those who have been gone for three months or more. The reality is stark and unsettling, and I firmly believe that many of these individuals have met with foul play. Somewhere out there, their killers walk among us, their secrets buried deep but never forgotten by the loved ones of those who have disappeared.

Police across Australia receive more than 38,000 missing person reports every year. That's one every 15 minutes.

It's a shocking statistic, and while most people – around 98 per cent – are found quickly, some never return, which has a devastating impact on family and friends, and ongoing significant implications.

The cases described in this book can make for tough reading. Families of missing people describe the experience as a form of mental torture that never goes away, because they never give up on searching for their missing loved one.

When someone you love disappears, it's not just a moment of panic, it's a lifetime of relentless searching and questioning. The reality is most of us can't begin to imagine the pain and torment of not knowing.

As I write, it's been more than 13,000 days since Mary Ashby last saw her daughter Debbie. Mary remembers the morning vividly. It was school holidays, Friday, 9 October 1987, just two days after Debbie's 16th birthday. Mary and her husband, Tony, set out on a day trip to Bowral, leaving their three daughters, of whom Debbie was the youngest, at home.

At around 1 pm, Debbie told her sisters she was going to a friend's house, and left the family home in Leumeah, in south-west Sydney, a place where she had always felt safe. It seemed like a typical teenage outing, but when Mary and Tony returned from Bowral their youngest daughter was not at home.

Dinnertime came and went without a word from Debbie. Panic set in, and Mary started calling Debbie's friends, desperately trying to locate her daughter. But no one had been in contact with the teenager. The night stretched into a torturous vigil, as Mary sat up hoping to hear a knock at the front door.

The next morning, still with no contact from Debbie, Mary headed straight to her local police station to report her daughter missing. The response she received shows just how differently missing person cases were handled back then. Mary was told to come back in 48 hours if Debbie hadn't returned. 'It happens all the time,' the cops said. 'We'll find them in three days, three weeks, three months or never.' These words, seemingly indifferent, became etched in Mary's mind, haunting her with the terrible possibility that she would never see her daughter again.

Two days after Debbie vanished, a glimmer of hope came in the form of a phone call. Debbie's sister Mechelle was at work when her boss approached her, saying there was a call for her. Mechelle picked up the phone in the office and heard Debbie's voice. 'Hi Shelly, it's Debbie. I'm okay.' But before Mechelle could ask where she was, the line went dead. That brief phone call was the last time the Ashby family had contact with Debbie.

Before her disappearance, Debbie had been going through a rebellious stage, facing difficulties at school, where she'd been singled out and bullied. Someone had even made threatening phone calls to her family home. The school had asked Mary to keep Debbie at home for her safety. These circumstances must have added to a growing sense of dread and confusion for a girl already dealing with the challenges of being a teenager.

The police were now on the lookout for Debbie, but no officer was specifically assigned to her case. Her photo had been circulated and cops would have been keeping an eye out while on patrol, but they had plenty of other police work to do.

Determined to find answers, Mary began to door-knock the local area, speaking to anyone who might have seen Debbie. One conversation with a local shopkeeper shook her to the core. The woman told Mary she remembered Debbie coming into the shop with a large wad of cash. Mary knew Debbie hadn't got it from home, and the mystery of the money lingered, adding another layer of fear and uncertainty.

Then, about a week after Debbie disappeared, another unsettling event occurred. Someone broke into the Ashbys' home and ransacked Debbie's room. Nothing was taken and police found no evidence linking the break-in to Debbie's disappearance, but the timing was too coincidental to ignore.

Had it been Debbie? Or had it been someone else, someone with a sinister motive? Mary's mind raced with possibilities, each one more terrifying than the last.

As the days turned into weeks and the weeks into months, the strain on Mary was immense. She began to lose her grip on reality. Once-simple tasks became insurmountable challenges. On one occasion, she found herself lost just 100 metres from home, unable to remember where she was going or how to get back. On another occasion, she was paralysed with fear when she discovered a large sum of money in her bag, convinced she had stolen it because she couldn't remember how it had got into her purse or why it was there.

Mary's descent into confusion and despair is typical of the emotional trauma families endure when a loved one goes missing. Like any family, the Ashbys were no strangers to drama and stress, but the uncertainty of not knowing what had happened to Debbie pushed them to the brink.

Despite police inquiries and public appeals in the media, Debbie's case, like many missing person cases, went cold. But Mary refused to give up. She stuck photos of Debbie on a large display board and began travelling around New South Wales. She would stop at shopping centres, where she'd speak to people in the hope of gathering information on Debbie's whereabouts. She was unwavering in her determination, driven by a mother's love and a desperate need for answers. She sought these answers in every face that passed by, every whisper of a clue, every shred of hope.

Debbie's case was the first missing person case I reported on, way back in 1992, and it left an indelible mark on me. I had just left the NSW Police Force and was working as a reporter on a tabloid current affairs show called *Hard Copy*.

Thirty-two years later, Debbie Ashby's story still haunts me. I've never been able to let go of the Sydney teenager's disappearance.

My career had begun in the wild 1980s on the gritty streets of Darlinghurst and Kings Cross, where, among many things, I dealt with countless cases of kids who'd run away from home. It was Debbie's case that inspired me to dedicate myself to finding missing people and giving a voice to the families left behind. I believe it's vital to seek answers for them.

Many of the runaways in Kings Cross came from dysfunctional families in which there wasn't always someone to love them, but Debbie was different. She had a loving family, whose pain at her disappearance was palpable, and who never gave up on trying to find her.

I think that's why Debbie's case touched me so deeply. I can still see the sadness etched in her mother's eyes, still hear her voice break when she spoke about Debbie. Things like that are hard to forget. I have covered hundreds more missing person cases over the years, but Debbie's case has always loomed large, and I have often thought about her family and how they've coped.

So in 2023, more than three decades since first reporting on Debbie's story, I decided to reach out to Mary. In all that time she had kept the same phone number, a lifeline she hoped Debbie might one day use to call home. Families of missing people grip tightly to the past in case their missing loved one is alive and decides to come home. Not only do they not change phone numbers, but often they also won't sell the family home, fearful that if their missing loved one returns one day, they'll knock on the door and find them gone.

Mary had finally and reluctantly sold the family home, but she hadn't moved far, staying in south-west Sydney in a neighbouring suburb. That connection to the area that Debbie was so familiar with was something Mary could never sever.

As I drove to Mary's house, I wondered how the years without Debbie might have been for the Ashby family. People try to move on but it's clear to me that they never can. The ghost of their missing loved one is there when they first wake up in the morning and there when they lie their head on their pillow to go to sleep. It's like a scar that only they can see.

When I turned into Mary's street, her home stood out from all the other neat red-brick houses, with its immaculate garden and pink roses lining the path to the front door.

I rang the bell and heard footsteps approach. Greeting Mary felt like stepping back in time. Her warm smile and soft voice were just as I remembered. We hugged and she led me through to the dining room, where Debbie's older sisters, Hayley and Mechelle, were waiting. Mary had prepared quite the feast. On the dining table was an assortment of pastries, a carrot cake, Italian cannoli, fruit, cold drinks and a pot of tea. It was a spread that spoke of hospitality and the hope for comfort in the midst of pain.

Our initial conversation was light, just small talk that barely touched on the reason I was there. Instead, we caught up on the years that had passed, but the reason for my visit loomed over everyone like a shadow. Talking about a missing loved one is never easy, but the Ashby family have endured the agony of recounting their story over and over, hoping that each time they did, it could lead to someone coming forward who might have answers.

Mary's voice trembled as she spoke of the milestones Debbie had missed – her sisters' weddings, the birth of nephews and nieces, the death of loved ones. 'Time doesn't heal,' she said, her voice breaking. 'It definitely doesn't. I've tried very hard to find closure over the years. When my husband died, we had a plot for him, and I bought two extras, one for me and one for Debbie, all in an attempt to get some sort of closure and accept that she's gone.'

As Mary recounted the events surrounding Debbie's disappearance, the details were as vivid as ever. Debbie had left without warning, and her absence had left an unfillable void. The weeks, months and years that had followed were a blur of fear, confusion and relentless searching. Mary's resilience had been nothing short of extraordinary. Despite the trauma, she had never given up hope.

For me, missing person cases are more than just a professional pursuit. They are a personal mission. The sadness that lingered in Mary's eyes, the pain that I still heard in her voice, and the raw emotions of the family revealed the trauma and anguish they have all endured. Mary's voice cracked under the weight of her emotions, and resonated with a depth of sorrow that was impossible to ignore. I still find it hard to listen to stories from heartbroken families, each word a testament to their enduring grief. It's something you never get used to.

'We travelled quite some distance, following leads that came in,' Mary recalled. 'We went to Nowra, up to Newcastle, following leads. I had a stand with posters of many missing people. We travelled around with that, and to the Easter Show – we went to the police stand with missing persons posters. I'd have been happy to find any missing person, but, of course, Debbie was my main focus.'

In the early 1990s, about four years after Debbie went missing, Mary received a tip that Debbie had been living in Nowra on the New South Wales South Coast and that she might even have a couple of children. Fuelled by hope, Mary, Tony and Hayley rushed to an address in Nowra. Tony had discharged himself from hospital to drive them there.

Mary described the moment to me as a mix of hope and dread. 'Hayley and I went to the front door, and I could hear a child behind it. I thought my heart was going to burst out of my chest. But when the door opened, it wasn't Debbie.'

Another time, three girls in Wollongong, south of Sydney, claimed that Debbie had died of a drug overdose. 'They were looking at Debbie's photo, they seemed really genuine and sure between themselves. They said Debbie had overdosed on drugs and was taken to the Royal North Shore Hospital where she died. We contacted Royal North Shore Hospital, but there was no record of an overdose in that timeframe. Another false lead.'

The emotional rollercoaster for Mary and her family was relentless, with moments of hope quickly dashed by disappointment. How they coped day after day remains a mystery to me. Yet they continued walking the streets and knocking on doors, searching for any clue that would lead them to Debbie.

'It was shattering at times,' Mary admitted, 'but while I was out there doing something, I wasn't just sitting back. It gave me a sense of purpose. It was good to at least be out there and not sitting back waiting to get feedback from the police. We were out there trying to find her.'

Mary's determination had no bounds. She and her daughter Hayley even followed up tips given to them by the police, who handed over pages of leads reported to Crime Stoppers for them to pursue. I'd never heard of this practice, but perhaps the police believed that the family, knowing Debbie better, would recognise small details that might otherwise be overlooked.

'Well, it was typical at that time, the police would actually ring and ask Mum to follow up on some of the leads,' Hayley explained. 'Of course, we really didn't have the investigative skills to ask the right questions, but we went to places we shouldn't have been. We visited the house of a prostitute living with her pimp. You don't think about your own safety at the time. But afterwards, in hindsight, you start to think, "Well, that may not have been the best decision for two females turning up at that location."'

Hayley and Mary visited the notorious red-light district of Kings Cross on numerous occasions, and even a women's prison, trying to find answers.

Hayley remembered one particularly eerie trip to Silverwater women's prison in Sydney's west. 'A neighbour had a friend who was a prison warden in that particular women's jail, and she told us there was a prisoner who looked very much like Debbie. So we decided to go there and see if it was Debbie, and it was quite scary. Mum and I were all dressed up, which, in hindsight, was ridiculous, but we were thinking that possibly we were going to see Debbie for the first time in years, and we were quite excited by this,' Hayley recalled. 'But when we got there it wasn't Debbie. The woman did look a lot like her, though. She said, "I knew you'd come one day. Everyone here thinks I'm Debbie." She even had newspaper clippings of every article about Debbie and she said she had been waiting for us to come.'

It was a huge letdown for Hayley and Mary. They had been so full of anticipation walking into the prison. They'd even taken gifts for the woman they hoped would be Debbie. However, despite the crushing disappointments, Mary and Hayley persisted. 'It was heartbreaking,' Mary said, 'but we had to keep going. We couldn't give up.'

As time went on, Mary began to think something terrible had happened to Debbie. When bodies were found in the Belanglo State Forest in the early 1990s, she became convinced that Debbie had been another victim of Ivan Milat, the notorious backpacker serial killer. 'They started finding the bodies in the forest and I was convinced they'd find her. I was convinced of it.'

Milat was convicted of murdering seven backpackers, but police believe there were many more victims. His game plan was to drive up and down the Hume Highway looking for hitchhikers to pick up, before taking them to Belanglo State Forest, where he would torture and kill them before burying their bodies in shallow graves covered with leaves and branches.

'I used to have nightmares about it when they started giving the details of what had happened. It was horrific. It was frightening,' Mary exclaimed.

Milat might have been active in the area where Debbie disappeared. When he was arrested in 1993, he lived just a ten-minute drive from Leumeah, where Debbie was last seen.

'So this is a really strong belief you have,' I said to Mary. 'Is it a mother's instinct?'

'Maybe,' Mary said. 'We know that Ivan Milat was active in his killings before those first bodies were found, and it's likely he could have been passing through Leumeah. I think it's a highly likely scenario. It's not something I want to be true, because then we know that something horrific happened to her, but unfortunately it is a possibility.'

In the months before Milat died of cancer in 2019, detectives interviewed him, hoping he would reveal the locations of other victims. They tried to appeal to his conscience and persuade him to come clean about whether there really were other victims. But Milat remained defiant, refusing to give any information.

'Do you think Debbie could be buried somewhere out there in Belanglo?' I asked Mary.

'Yes, definitely,' she replied. 'I've been to Belanglo. It's horrible, but I had to go, and I went down when they had the memorial service for the English girls.'

As Mary stood there with other mourners at the service, praying for the British backpackers Caroline Clarke and Joanne Walters, whose bodies were the first to be discovered, she wondered if Milat's killing fields might also hold the unmarked grave of her own daughter.

* * *

For the families of missing people, the prospect of finding out what happened to their loved one is a double-edged sword because there's a high likelihood that the missing person is deceased, and if that is confirmed it is shattering. I asked Mary if that was something she would want to know, or whether she would prefer to hold on to hope.

'My position is, I would want to know,' Mary responded. 'Hope … hope can cripple you, and hope has crippled me at times. If you know what you're dealing with, you can cope with it, no matter how difficult, so you are not going backwards and forwards all the time.'

Letting go of the past can be impossible. Holding on to memories can be like wrapping yourself in your favourite blanket. It's comforting and safe.

The four of us moved to a small table in Mary's kitchen, where Mary had laid out photos of Debbie alongside newspaper clippings and some of her missing daughter's personal possessions. She picked up an old school photo of Debbie and showed it to me. The teenager's smile was ambiguous – a hint of happiness mixed with something else, something deeper and perhaps more troubling.

Mary also showed me a leather strap Debbie had made and a T-shirt with Debbie's photo emblazoned on the front. Mary had worn it when she travelled around the state looking for her daughter. She had kept Debbie's diaries, which were filled with entries about boys she liked and things she was doing. These items were priceless reminders of Debbie, and Mary would never part with them.

'It's difficult to let go of things that remind you of happier times,' Mary says. 'I kept her clothes for about 20 years. Eventually, I donated them to a women's refuge, where a lady came in and she had absolutely nothing – she had to flee her home and she was the same size as Debbie, and she needed them.'

Mechelle and Hayley also had cherished mementos of their sister. Mechelle has given her daughter the same middle name as Debbie: Marie.

Hayley's connection to Debbie was something simple yet priceless. 'It's not really anything worth any money, but it's really a sentimental thing,' she explained. 'It's something that was special to Debbie. Back in the 1980s it was quite common to have these little cardboard boxes of talcum powder with a powder puff, and I still have one that belonged to Debbie. It's on my bedside table, a small reminder of her.'

The families left behind hold on to anything because there's a gaping hole in their hearts. Sometimes that can lead them to ask a long list of what-ifs and to grapple with feelings of guilt. I asked Mary if she thought Debbie might have started a new life and found it too difficult to come back.

'I have thought that many, many times. It would be harder the longer it goes on – the more difficult it would be,' Mary conceded. 'I had a letter published in one of the magazines where I said I might have made it difficult for Debbie to come home because I constantly kept her in the media. I did everything I could to make sure her picture was out there all the time. In hindsight, I'm not sure I would do that again.'

I tried to reassure Mary that what she did was what any loving mother would have done to find her missing child, but I don't think I succeeded. I imagine part of her guilt would be around the feeling that something bad could have befallen Debbie and she'd failed to protect her. But Mary didn't need to feel guilty; her unwavering determination to find Debbie was nothing short of extraordinary, and it continues today.

In 1997, a coronial inquest before Deputy State Coroner Carl Milovanovich made the distressing finding that Debbie was deceased. Police put missing person cases before coroners who then formally determine whether the person is alive or dead.

While the coroner found that Debbie was most likely deceased, the precise date, place and cause of her death were undetermined. The coroner's decision, while expected, was still shattering. For the first time, Mary had to confront her worst fear: that she would most likely never see Debbie alive again.

Mary kept a copy of the coroner's report and she showed me a paragraph that haunts her every day. It reads: 'The findings will be that Debbie Marie Ashby is deceased. That she died after Sunday, 11 October 1987. As to the precise date and place of her death or the manner and cause of her death, from the evidence adduced, I am unable to say.'

All those years of driving around the state, showing photos of her daughter, knocking on strangers' doors, following up every lead and tip that came in and putting herself in danger – was that all for nothing?

To this day, Debbie's disappearance remains a mystery. Her family continue to search for answers, hoping that some day they will find out what happened to her.

'It's really important for Mum to have some answers,' Hayley said. 'As a mother, you never stop thinking about it, you never stop worrying about it, and it's difficult to get on with your life.'

Mary's hope endures, even as she confronts the possibility that Debbie might have been a victim of Ivan Milat. 'Till the day he died I hoped he would speak up because there's a big part of me that still thinks maybe that he was involved.'

I never believed that Milat would break his silence and confess to other killings. I mean let's face it, he was a coward, and it takes guts to admit you've done something terrible. For over two decades, right up until he died in October 2019, the confines of prison dictated his every move. In jail he was told when to wake up, sleep, shower and eat. Yet, amidst this regimented existence, he clung to one vestige of control: the knowledge of his other crimes and his victims' whereabouts. By keeping these secrets and taking them to the grave, the cruel killer wielded power even in death, continuing to torment the families of his victims with unending grief, uncertainty, pain and suffering.

Milat's death left Mary with a dissatisfying sense of things unresolved, as it did dozens of other families like hers.

If Mary's suspicions about Milat are correct and he did murder Debbie, it opens a Pandora's box of grim possibilities.

Milat came from a large family, and he liked to brag and revel in notoriety. So there's a chance that someone close to him knows something, a piece of the puzzle they've been withholding all these years.

NSW Police told me there is no evidence linking Ivan Milat to Debbie's disappearance, but they cannot exclude the possibility that he was involved. There is no evidence to show that Milat made his victims phone home.

But if it wasn't Ivan Milat, then who was responsible for Debbie's disappearance? And are they still out there?

The truth about Debbie's fate may never be known. The unanswered questions and relentless search for answers continue to haunt Mary and her family, leaving them in a perpetual state of grief and uncertainty. The mystery of Debbie's disappearance remains a dark cloud hanging over their lives, casting a shadow that refuses to lift.

***

Decades after Debbie vanished, a potential breakthrough emerged. Following the release of my podcast episode and a feature in the newspapers on 25 May 2023, a man named Bob Mimid came forward with a remarkable claim.

Bob recalled seeing a woman he believes to be Debbie in Brisbane around 12 years ago. He regularly spotted her on Thursdays, sitting on the steps of Woolworths at Buranda Village on Ipswich Road with a group of other women, waiting for the chemist to open so they could collect methadone. A local resident told Bob that this woman had run away from Sydney and was using her middle name, Marie.

After hearing my podcast, Bob searched online for images of Debbie Ashby and became convinced she was the same person he'd seen all those years before. He told me he'd reported his findings to both Queensland and NSW Police, but he said his information was met with indifference.

Determined to verify his claim, I contacted the Buranda Village chemist. A pharmacist confirmed that methadone had been dispensed from there in the past, before the current owners had taken over and discontinued the practice.

I passed this new lead on to Debbie's mother, Mary, who took the information to Campbelltown Police. 'We're trying not to get our hopes too high,' she told me, 'but this needs to be followed up.'

She is right! I believe police could make inquiries with Queensland Health to find out if a Marie or Debbie Ashby was ever registered to be on the methadone program. It's not that long ago, and the records should still exist.

At the time of writing, Bob Mimid has yet to be contacted by NSW Police.

***

Do you know what happened to Debbie Ashby?

Someone, somewhere, holds the key to this mystery. Debbie would be 52 years old today. She is described as 160 centimetres tall, with a slim build, brown hair, brown eyes and a fair complexion. There is a $100,000 reward for information about Debbie's disappearance.

2

A Boy Called Daniel

Daniel Morcombe

Sunday, 7 December 2003 began like any other summer day on Queensland's Sunshine Coast. Daniel Morcombe, a bright-eyed 13-year-old with an angelic smile, was heading out to get a haircut and to buy Christmas presents for his family at Maroochydore's Sunshine Plaza shopping centre. He left his family's Palmwoods home excited and with a spring in his step, looking forward to the festive season and the joy it would bring.

But that joy was not to be. After walking a kilometre to the bus stop under the Kiel Mountain Road overpass on the Nambour Connection Road, Daniel vanished, never to

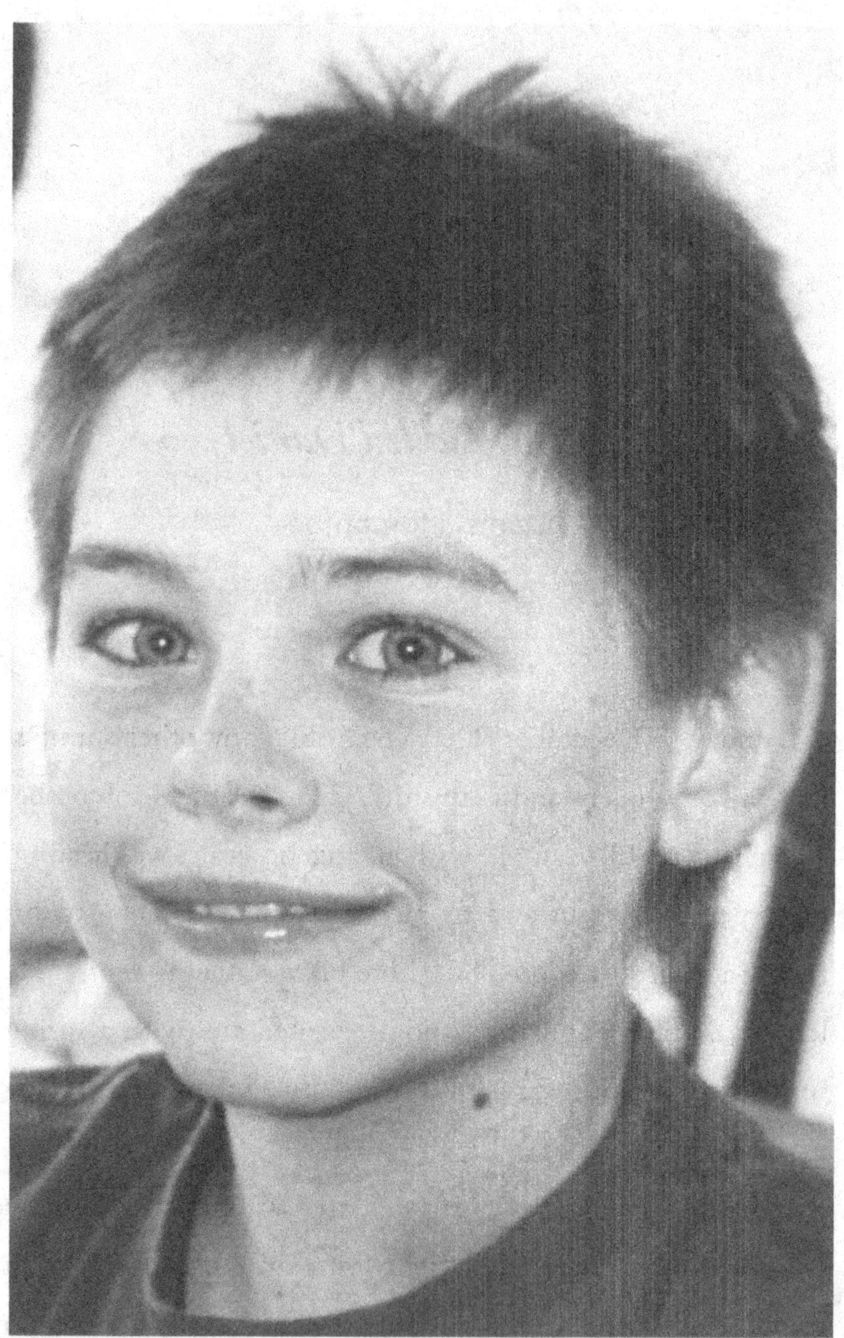

Daniel Morcombe

return. He was last seen at 2.10 pm, wearing a red T-shirt and waiting for a bus. His disappearance sparked a national outpouring of grief and led to the biggest investigation in Queensland Police history.

Detective Superintendent John Maloney led the investigation, interviewing more than 500 people and tirelessly following up over 16,000 individual leads. 'Every week we get a telephone call or information from Crime Stoppers with new areas to investigate,' he said early in the investigation, reflecting on his frustration at dead ends and false leads. Despite the police effort and an extensive media blitz following an unprecedented public awareness campaign launched by Daniel's parents, at that point the mystery of Daniel's disappearance remained unsolved.

I first interviewed the Morcombe family in early 2004, just weeks after Daniel vanished, when I was working as a reporter for a nightly television current affairs program.

Denise told me she vividly remembered the morning when she last saw Daniel. 'The boys got up and had breakfast. I remember putting the clothes out on the line. Daniel said to me, "Do you know what Dad bought you from a magazine?" I said, "No, I don't." I remember him walking down the path to go to the bus stop, and that was it.'

With heartbreaking precision, Denise could recount the details of what apparently happened next. 'Danny came down [to the bus stop] about half past one ... He was waiting to catch a bus and to buy some Christmas presents. About a kilometre down the road, a bus was broken down but Daniel couldn't see that. He'd been waiting ... for about 40 minutes. At ten past two a replacement bus drove past Daniel and didn't stop. Three minutes later, another bus came by and Daniel had disappeared. He wasn't ... at the bus stop.'

A broken-down bus, another bus that didn't stop: cruel twists of fate that conspired against a young boy. Those three lost minutes devastated the Morcombe family and became forever etched in their memories.

In the days that followed Daniel's disappearance, Bruce and Denise decided to walk the path Daniel took from home to the bus stop, hoping to find any clues. 'We looked in the shrubs to see if we could find anything,' Denise recalled.

Bruce initially thought Daniel might have been the victim of a hit-and-run accident. 'Maybe a car had clipped him or something,' Bruce said to Denise. 'Let's find what's left of the poor bugger and deal with it then.'

As days turned to weeks then months then years, any hope of finding Daniel alive faded. 'Someone has an answer. Just come forward with an answer for us,' Bruce would plead in the media.

For Bruce and Denise Morcombe, the pain of their son's disappearance was a wound that never healed. 'Crimes against children are the worst of the worst,' Bruce said, his voice thick with emotion. The family, including Daniel's twin, Bradley, and his older brother, Dean, became caught up in a relentless cycle of hope and despair.

'We quickly realised that the only way to improve from worse to better was to hold the family unit together as best we could,' Bruce said to me once, his eyes betraying the deep sadness he tried to hide. But despite the occasional laughs and good times, there was always a sense of something missing.

'We're always missing one,' Denise said, her voice a poignant reminder of their loss.

On one occasion when I was at their place, we filmed a sequence of the family sitting down for dinner. It was a scene that brought me to tears. As the family took their seats around the dining table, a lone chair where Daniel should have been sitting remained empty. Although it was unoccupied, I caught each family member glancing towards it, as if they had a vain hope Daniel would suddenly appear.

Bradley, Daniel's twin, felt the absence most acutely. 'It's torn us all apart and it's hurting everyone,' he admitted when I spoke to him four years after Daniel disappeared. His words echoed the pain that had become a constant companion. 'It's affected me a lot because Dean's moved out of home, and it's as if I'm a single child now.'

Dean coped by getting tattoos, dedicating his left arm to his little brother. 'The left arm's for him,' he explained. 'You've got "never forgotten", "goodbye" and a cross with three candles – two lit, one's out. It reminds me of Daniel's birthday after he disappeared. There were three candles and one of them kept going out.'

Denise and Bruce would often visit the bus stop, where they had a stone memorial built for their son. They would spend hours cleaning the plaque about Daniel and picking up old flowers and letters left by well-wishers. Among the tributes were small plastic toys and bags of sweets. 'Well, I probably drive past here every day or every second day,' Denise said. 'It's not where Daniel is. He's not buried here, but to me it's just the last spot that we know where he was.'

It's the not knowing that tears families apart. I think it's the most devastating kind of loss – in some ways even worse than death – because you have no idea if your loved one is alive or dead, suffering or at peace. When someone dies you have a funeral, and a place to visit and pay your respects, but with a missing person you have none of that.

Bruce Morcombe once described having a missing loved one as a nightmare you never wake up from. 'It's a continuous feeling of loss and hopelessness that just goes on and on,' he told me. It's an emotional form of torture and it never gets easier, because families never give up.

I recall Bruce telling me once that the thing he found most difficult to deal with was the unrelenting struggle to cope with the million different scenarios about Daniel's fate that would flood his head and cause him to go to dark places. 'The worst thing that I live with is to do with the not knowing,' he said. 'Unfortunately, Daniel's case is often linked with paedophile activity, and you just wonder what the hours and the days brought for him.'

The pain of remembering the nightmare was unbearable, but they had to learn to live with it. 'You still have those memories,' Bruce told me. 'He never made his fourteenth birthday and it's just such a cruel way to leave a sentence unanswered, you know? We just don't have an end to it, and that's what we're working so hard to do, to find Danny's remains and lay the poor bugger to rest.'

There was a moment during the last interview that I did with the Morcombes that I will never forget. It was a moment overwhelmed with heartbreak, grief, anguish and sorrow. It's deeply ingrained in my mind, and whenever I think about it, I feel like I've been punched in the stomach and the wind has been knocked out of me.

I was standing in the Morcombe's carport watching Bruce and Denise do what no parent should ever have to do: pack up and store their missing child's clothes and belongings. For four years they'd kept Daniel's room the same as it had been the day he vanished, everything in its place, untouched. Finally, they had mustered the strength to pack Daniel's belongings into the back of the family van and take them to a storage unit.

I followed their car to the nearby storage facility, then helped them move the large plastic tubs and cardboard boxes full of Daniel's things. As we put down the last of the boxes, I asked Denise why she was keeping Daniel's clothes, because even if he did return home one day, he would have grown out of them.

Denise thought for a moment, then gave me an answer that demonstrated the power of a mother's love and her determination to find the truth. 'For the moment, we're just in limbo.' She paused before going on. 'We don't know whether he's dead or alive. We hear reports of overseas children that have been found after four, five or six years after they went missing, and that's what we keep hoping for, but until we've actually got that answer, until the police can physically tell me they've found Daniel's remains, I don't think that I can believe that he is dead.'

As I stood next to Denise outside the entrance to the storage unit, taking in her words, my attention was drawn to Bruce, who had stepped out of the back of the unit. 'And this is what's waiting for the bastard who took Daniel,' he snarled, holding up a dark-coloured noose. In his other hand he held a large sheet of tin on which he'd painted a message for whoever took Daniel: 'Swing, you bastard. Justice will be done.'

At that moment I had no doubt that if Bruce got his hands on the person who abducted Daniel, he would string them up a tree. And you know what? If I were in Bruce's position, I would do the same thing. Crimes against children are the worst of the worst, and those who commit them deserve no sympathy.

I asked Bruce what he intended to do with the noose and threatening sign, and he said that originally he'd wanted to hang them both under the bridge at the bus stop where Daniel was last seen, but after further consideration he'd decided against this very public display, because he didn't want people to think he was a nutter who had lost the plot.

However, he had decided to keep the noose and sign as motivation. He told me he came up with the slogan 'Don't waste your pain': four symbolic words he would use to channel all his energy into finding his son's killer.

Everyone affected by a loved one's disappearance reacts differently and deals with the situation in their own way. From the beginning, Bruce had conceded that Daniel would not be found alive. He told me this the first time I met him. He was convinced that his son was dead, and he was firm in that belief. Denise, on the other hand, held on to what I would describe as eternal hope, adamant that she would see Daniel alive again. Maybe she just didn't want to face the horrible possibility that Daniel was dead.

Many families of the missing suffer what is called 'ambiguous loss', a term coined by American educator and researcher Dr Pauline Boss, who spent decades studying family stress. At its core, ambiguous loss is all about a lack of resolution. Families of missing people don't know if their loved one is alive or dead or where their loved one's remains are located. There is no closure around the loss, so they may continue to hope that the missing person will return.

I could never imagine the pain that families of missing people like the Morcombes feel, nor the strength it must have taken that day for Bruce and Denise to pack up Daniel's short life. Families hold on to possessions for dear life because they're reminders of their loved one. Their smell on an item of clothing, an old football they spent hours kicking or a piece of jewellery you gave them on a special occasion.

We left the storage unit that day and returned to the Morcombe's home, where Bruce pointed out some animals in a fenced yard. 'There are certain things you can't leave behind, and one of those, of course, is his horse. It was probably his most prized possession,' Bruce told me fondly. Daniel's horse, called Bullett, remained in the family as a cherished connection to their lost son and brother. 'It was something that comforted him,' Bruce said. 'When you'd roused on him, you wondered where he was and he'd be down talking to his horse. [Bullet] always talks to you; he grunts and nays and it's as though Danny's talking to us,' Bruce said, smiling. 'If we left him behind it's as though we're leaving Danny behind, so he's always coming with us.'

Without doubt the Morcombe family's most treasured possessions are the precious home movies that provide glimpses of happier times. On one occasion, we sat in the lounge room and Bruce played a video of a young Daniel with a beaming smile, roaring with laughter as he celebrated his shared birthday with Bradley. They splash around in a swimming pool, looking so happy. These moments caught on tape are vivid reminders of that time when the family was whole.

* * *

For nearly eight years the Morcombe family struggled with the trauma of not knowing. It sounds like a long time, but many other families of missing people spend a lifetime waiting for answers they never get. A family's love has no expiry date, so the suffering can last forever.

But on 13 August 2011, nearly eight years after Daniel vanished from that bus stop, the Morcombe family finally got some form of closure. An elaborate undercover police sting that was carried out across two states had trapped Brett Peter Cowan and he was arrested and charged with Daniel's murder.

During the police operation, Cowan was secretly recorded confessing to abducting and killing Daniel. 'Yeah, okay, you know, yeah, I did it,' Cowan said matter of factly, before he described luring Daniel into his car, driving him to an isolated spot, pulling his pants down then choking him.

Cowan had been a suspect from the beginning, but the cops hadn't had enough evidence to arrest him for Daniel's abduction until a coronial inquest into Daniel's disappearance in 2010 named him as a person of interest.

In a complex police operation, an undercover cop befriended Cowan. He introduced Cowan to his 'friends', who were supposedly part of an organised crime gang but were in fact other undercover police. With promises of easy money to be made, Cowan got sucked in.

Over several months Cowan was led to believe that he could become an important cog in the gang once he proved his loyalty. In an attempt to convince his new friends that he could be trusted, Cowan provided a complete confession to an undercover cop, which has been recounted in the book *Where is Daniel? The Family's Story*, by Bruce and Denise Morcombe. The following extract highlights the vile and violent nature of his crime. It makes for tough reading. It's a frightening and disturbing insight into the mind of a vile child molester and killer.

> 'There was no struggle, no fucking screaming and shouting – nothing. He willingly got into my car. I sat up against the wall, you know, waitin', and um, yeah, when,

um the bus drove past, he was like "Oh fuck, what am I gonna do?" and I offered him a lift. Came and got in the car and we left. Went back the same way.'

'And where'd he sit?' asked the undercover cop.

'Front seat. If there was anything found in the car, I wouldn't be sitting here with youse now.'

Cowan describes Daniel as 'fucking cute'. Asked what Daniel was wearing the day he enticed him into his car, Cowan replied, 'Red shirt, blue pants, shoes and socks.'

'Where was he going?' probed the undercover cop.

'Going to get a haircut, going into Sunshine Plaza. I told him I'd give him a lift but I had no intention of taking him to the shopping centre.'

'What were you thinking?' pressed the cop.

'I don't really know what I was thinking. I'm an opportunistic offender.'

Cowan's meticulous description of how he carried out his ghastly crime indicated to me that he had done this before. While it was a crime of opportunity – Cowan happened to be driving by as Daniel waited at the bus stop – he acted immediately when presented with a chance set of circumstances and relied on a tried and tested method.

Serial offenders often have a distinct way of carrying out their crimes. Cops call it their 'modus operandi', 'method of operation' or simply 'MO'.

Cowan went on to describe how he told Daniel he had to quickly 'duck home' to let his missus know what was going on. He openly admitted he had no intention of going 'anywhere near my wife'. He talked about turning off the road and heading into the bush, where he was going to take Daniel to an old abandoned building and abuse the boy. But things suddenly went very wrong.

Cowan's chilling and detailed description of what happened to Daniel was recorded on a hidden camera that was played at his trial in 2014.

'That's where I thought he was going to run, and my arm went around his neck and I choked him out,' Cowan said. 'I actually felt that break in there, so, like, in that bone thing. I felt that snap in me arm when I pushed it in below the Adam's apple.'

On the recording, the killer's voice is soft and nonchalant, as if he is describing nothing significant. His inability to recognise the horror of what he did and Daniel's obvious distress before he was killed marks him as a perverted psychopath.

The brilliance of the undercover cop who managed to trap Cowan into making a full confession should never be underestimated, because it took a murderous paedophile off the streets.

Other audio evidence recorded Cowan taking undercover police to bushland where he had dumped the missing boy's body. Police will take a crook who's in custody back to the scene of the crime and have them recount what they did. It allows police to conduct a systematic examination of the scene and a step-by-step analysis of what took place.

A week after Cowan's arrest, on 21 August 2011, nearly nine years after Daniel disappeared, three human bones were discovered at the Glass House Mountains in the rugged hinterland of Queensland's Sunshine Coast. As well, a pair of shoes and other items were found almost exactly where Cowan had said they would be. Eventually, 17 bones were found, with DNA matching that found on Daniel's toothbrush.

On 13 March 2014, in Brisbane's Supreme Court, Brett Peter Cowan was found guilty of indecently dealing with Daniel Morcombe, murdering him and interfering with his corpse. He was sentenced to life in jail with a non-parole period of 20 years.

Sentencing Cowan, Justice Roslyn Atkinson said his crime was 'entirely abhorrent'. 'You didn't look like a monster, you didn't look like a paedophile, you looked like an ordinary person,' she said. 'You knew if he ran away, you'd be caught. So you killed him. Everything you did to that boy is horrific and disgraceful. I've seen no evidence in the months you've been in this court that you ever felt any remorse for what you did. You have tragically and pointlessly snuffed out a young life.'

Bruce and Denise Morcombe declined to attend the sentencing of the man who killed their son. It was the final chapter in this tragic story, and while the Morcombes never saw their son and brother again, they got an ending, and Daniel was brought home. They were able to lay their boy to rest, hold a service for him, say goodbye, mourn his loss and end the constant torment of not knowing his fate.

I cannot imagine the relief Daniel's family must have experienced to finally have a definitive answer about what happened to him. Only then could they really begin to grieve.

Since returning Daniel home, his parents and brothers have had the comfort of being able to visit him at his resting place, where they can pay their respects.

However, for thousands of other families, the nightmare of never knowing continues. The dark cloud of uncertainty hangs over them. Each day is a new chapter in their endless, heart-wrenching search for answers.

***

After Cowan's sentencing, the Morcombes could have cocooned themselves from the world, but they didn't. Determined that no other child should suffer the same tragic fate as their son, Bruce and Denise continued to work hard on the foundation they had established in 2005, just two years after their precious boy disappeared.

The Daniel Morcombe Foundation has given them a focus and a mission to protect children. They work tirelessly to promote child safety and prevent other children from being abducted. 'It's a small price to save a child,' Denise said. 'Even if it only saves one child, it's worth it.'

Through their pain, the Morcombes found a purpose, transforming their tragedy into a beacon of hope for others. Daniel's spirit lives on, not just in their hearts, but also in the lives they continue to touch through the foundation. And in this way, the Morcombes have honoured their son's memory, ensuring that his story will never be forgotten.

3

A Life Interrupted

Lorrin Whitehead

I read a book called *The Invisible Backpack of Grief*, and I feel that's exactly what having a missing loved one is like. You constantly wear this grief on your back, and some days it's as heavy as the first days you put it on, and the first day that it happened.

Amelia Grozdanovski

The story of 43-year-old Lorrin Whitehead is a chilling enigma. A devoted mother of five, Lorrin vanished without a trace, leaving behind a shattered family and questions of who, what, where, when and why.

Lorrin Whitehead

Lorrin's life had never been easy, but she was a fighter who always got through the toughest of times. Then just when it seemed like she was finally finding her feet, she was gone.

In 2023, as I drove to Newcastle, north of Sydney, to speak to Amelia Grozdanovski, Lorrin's eldest child, the thought of Amelia's grief really sat with me. Amelia was only 19 when her mother disappeared, and she had the weight of the world thrust upon her. Her mother's disappearance in 2013 propelled her into adulthood and she was suddenly responsible for helping to look after her four younger siblings. Now, a decade later, she had become a nurse, a wife and a mother, three roles she embraced while still trying to understand the inexplicable loss of her mum.

Lorrin was selfless, giving and brave, traits Amelia had to quickly adopt. It was a case of sink or swim and, like her mother, Amelia fought hard to keep her head above water. I wanted to learn all I could about Lorrin, in particular her emotional and mental state leading up to her disappearance.

Amelia's home was in a relatively new estate that was still growing. Tradies' utes lined the streets and the sounds of hammering and power tools filled the air. As I parked in Amelia's driveway, I was struck by how normal it all seemed. There was nothing to suggest the tragedy that had shaped her life.

Amelia met me at the door, telling me her husband, Chris, was putting their baby, Ayla, to sleep. Her face was a mask of composure, but I sensed she was nervous. Years of unresolved pain were etched into her face, and her eyes were full of sadness and loss.

Once inside, we sat at the dining table, speaking in hushed tones as we waited for Chris to emerge from the bedroom with the thumbs-up. When he finally did, Amelia took a deep breath and began her story.

'My name is Amelia,' she said softly, her voice quavering. 'I'm the eldest daughter of Lorrin Jane Whitehead, also known as Lorrin Kaiser. My mum went missing back on Friday, 8 February 2013. It's been ten years now – I never thought I'd be saying that out loud.' Amelia paused, clearly struggling with the enormity of it all. 'Lorrin was my mum. We had a very normal family, at least that's what we thought. We lived in Bannockburn, a small town about an hour and a half south of Melbourne. That's where she was last seen.'

A lot of families of missing people feel guilty, and Amelia was no different. 'I think the hardest part,' she said before swallowing hard, 'is the guilt. Not guilt that she went missing, but guilt that I'm not doing more to find her. I constantly wonder if she's safe, if she's warm, if she's fed, if she's locked up somewhere. I'm a nurse, I'm a mum and a wife. I'm supposed to fix things, to make them better. But I can't fix this.'

Amelia's guilt resonated deeply with me. Many families of missing people replay events over and over, wondering what they could have done differently, what they could have said, what warning signs they might have missed.

The week before her mum vanished, Amelia had planned to meet her for their regular Wednesday coffee date, but she got sick and ended up in hospital because, like Lorrin, Amelia is diabetic. She messaged Lorrin to cancel, planning to reschedule for the following Monday, 11 February, but Lorrin never responded.

On the Monday, when Amelia still had not heard from her mum, she started to worry. Then came a call from Lorrin's boss, Norm Baker. Lorrin had not shown up for work.

Amelia's heart sank. She knew instantly that something was terribly wrong. Her younger siblings were at their father's house that week so she knew her mum was home alone. She rushed to her mother's house, dreading what she might find. She rang Norm to tell him what she was doing. He told her he would meet her there but to not go inside until he arrived.

'I pulled up to the house and the front door was open, the garage was open and everything was open,' Amelia recounted. 'I was standing on the driveway, pacing backwards and forwards wanting to go inside. Obviously, I waited for Norm to get there. Then Norm got there and searched the house and he said, "It's empty."'

Amelia described the scene inside the house as 'chaotic'. Lorrin's belongings were strewn across her bed – her purse, her life-saving insulin, her handbag, everything laid out as if she'd been preparing to leave. But she hadn't taken any of it. In the kitchen, a broken fruit bowl lay on the floor with peaches rotting in the middle of the mess. The sink was piled high with dirty dishes. Amelia told me her mum was a clean freak, and this scene of chaos raised alarm bells.

'It was all off. Everything felt off,' she stressed to me. 'Mum was a stickler for security, a single female living alone, so seeing everything open, I knew something was wrong.' Amelia's voice was laced with heartache. 'I told Norm, "We need to call the police," and we did. Bannockburn police came and they took a statement and looked at the house.'

Police didn't initially treat Lorrin's disappearance as suspicious. It wasn't until months later that the house was forensically examined. By then, any evidence that might have pointed to foul play or the presence of someone else in the house was long gone.

When I thought of the scene Amelia described inside her mother's house, I was troubled by the fruit bowl found in pieces on the kitchen floor. Did Lorrin drop it accidentally, or was it broken during a struggle with someone?

Remember, Lorrin's phone, handbag and, most critically, her insulin pens were left behind but, curiously, her computer and iPad were missing. It was an odd detail, and one that made me wonder whether someone else had been with Lorrin that day, someone who had taken the devices for a reason. I am theorising here, but what if there was something on the electronic devices that whoever took them did not want the police and Lorrin's family to find?

The police concluded that there were no suspicious circumstances and that Lorrin had left on her own. But Amelia was not so sure. She feared her mother had met a violent and tragic end at the hands of someone else, someone Lorrin knew.

I wanted to try to understand how the police who had initially assessed Lorrin's disappearance had come to the conclusion that there was nothing suspicious surrounding her case. So I reached out to the detective who is in charge of the matter, Detective Senior Constable Tim Robinson of Victoria Police.

'When someone goes missing such as Lorrin, we don't know a great deal about them in the initial report,' Tim told me. 'And then there's a number of circumstances that dictate whether it goes to a suspicious missing person – in this instance it wasn't – or whether it's what I would say is a routine missing person investigation.'

Police can only act on evidence, and with no obvious smoking gun in the house, they concluded that Lorrin had walked out the door on her own. I asked Tim what the police knew about Lorrin's last movements on Friday, 8 February, the day she went missing. 'Lorrin worked at a business in Geelong and she finished work at about three in the afternoon,' he told me. 'She attended Bannockburn, where she withdrew some money from an ATM. At about 4.30 pm she was observed by a neighbour to leave her house.'

Twenty-five minutes after leaving through her front gate, Lorrin was seen entering the Bannockburn Safeway supermarket, which was about 2 kilometres from her house. She was seen on the store's security cameras buying a bottle of water, a Hallmark card and a pen. It was the last time anyone saw her.

A few days later, a card addressed to Lorrin's kids showed up in the mailbox of Lorrin's ex-husband, Teo Kaiser. It was the last tangible trace of Lorrin. She hasn't been seen or heard from since.

There were markings on the card suggesting it had been processed by a mail centre and that it had been dropped off by regular post on Wednesday, 13 February, five days after Lorrin went missing.

On the front of the card was a photo of a smiley face drawn in the sand and the words: 'Don't cry because it's over. Smile because it happened.' Inside, the card was blank; nothing was written there. I asked Tim if police had carried out handwriting and forensic tests on the card and the envelope it came in. 'In relation to the handwriting, the sample was too small to definitely make those comparisons. The letter and the stamp and the adhesive on the back was DNA tested, with that coming back being attributable to Lorrin,' he confirmed.

The card sounded like a final farewell, so police launched a search, worried that Lorrin had taken her own life. 'We had ground searches and searches involving the air wing,' Tim said. 'We had specialists search heavily wooded and grassed areas, waterways and train lines, but we just haven't been able to get that piece of information that's helped us to identify where Lorrin is.'

Two days after the card arrived, it was Lorrin's turn to pick up her children from school and have them for the weekend, as per the custody agreement with her ex-husband, Teo. Amelia went to the school together with her grandparents Joan and Wayne, who had flown down from Queensland. They were hoping that Lorrin would turn up. Amelia told me they waited with nervous anticipation, staring at every car that drove by or was parked nearby. They studied every woman they saw, wishing it were Lorrin. 'Everyone was just holding their breath, and I remember it getting to 4.30 pm and I said, "She's not coming,"' Amelia recalled.

It's true that Lorrin was a woman who had battled difficult times. Being a mother of five has its trials and tribulations, but she loved the role. She had battled cancer and survived, and then found herself embroiled in a bitter divorce. It may have seemed that the weight of the world was unbearable, but those close to her insisted that she was thriving, that she was reclaiming her life, making plans for the future, and appeared happier than ever. And then she vanished.

'She was the best I'd seen her in a long time,' Amelia said. 'In the months leading up, her court order was settled with my stepdad. They'd finally set up custody agreements. She was planning, studying, looking at new jobs. We were planning a mother–daughter trip. Things were good. She was on the mend.'

The weekend before she disappeared, Lorrin spent time with her best friend Louise Anderson. When I met Louise she recalled their weekend together with a fondness that seemed almost surreal given what happened soon after. 'It was such a light-hearted weekend,' Louise told me. 'I remember thinking, *Gosh, Lorrin's in a good place.* She was such good company. The weight had lifted off her shoulders. I just don't understand. She looked and sounded so good. Was there something going on? I don't know. We just talked the whole weekend, but there was nothing deep about any of the discussions that stands out in my mind.'

Louise's recollection of their time together painted a picture of a woman who was anything but suicidal. Yet the following Monday everything changed when Louise received a frantic phone call from Amelia, telling her that Lorrin was missing. 'I couldn't believe it,' Louise said. As she told me about that day, she seemed to still be in disbelief, the memory still raw. 'I remember feeling sick to my stomach. My first gut instinct was: *What's Teo done?* It was the only thing that made sense.'

Louise's suspicion had no basis to it. Lorrin's ex-husband had been a source of stress in Lorrin's life but Detective

Robinson told me there was no evidence linking Teo to Lorrin's disappearance, and Teo was not a person of interest in the case.

Police have officially cleared Teo, and there is no suggestion made here that he had any involvement in Lorrin's disappearance, but this is what happens when someone goes missing. Those closest to the missing person are put under the microscope so they can be eliminated from the investigation, and people start to speculate and point the finger.

When I reached out to Teo, I was met with a wall of silence. He declined to participate in my podcast, citing his right to privacy, but not before he shared his belief that Lorrin might have succumbed to her mental health struggles and possibly taken her own life, or started afresh somewhere far from the life she once knew.

But Louise, Lorrin's best friend, completely dismisses Teo's theories. 'At the time of her disappearance, she didn't have the kids for that week, so when the police asked me if I thought she could have done that to herself, I said no. If she needed a break, she'd have gone away for the week and come back when she had the kids. The children would have drawn her back.'

Lorrin's parents, Joan and Wayne, are also adamant that their daughter would never abandon her young family. Though

Amelia was 19 when her mum disappeared, her siblings were much younger. Megan was 13, Rachel 12, Arnold 11 and Quade just 9 years old. It's inconceivable to me, after all I have learned about Lorrin, that she would turn her back on them all.

'Lorrin existed for her family,' Joan told me when we met, her voice cracking with emotion. 'Lorrin was a loving, caring mother and a loving, caring daughter. Her main concern was her children. Everything she did was for them.'

When I asked Wayne if he thought Lorrin might still be alive, he hesitated before answering. 'I don't think so. We live in hope and we look out every train window and every bus window hoping we may see her, but we haven't had any luck with that at all, so I doubt it.'

Joan said that Lorrin's disappearance had created a sadness and grief that was all-encompassing. 'It's extremely difficult because you never go to bed without thinking about them, and you wake up most mornings and you're always wondering. It doesn't go away.'

Wayne agreed, telling me that although he and Joan had moved on with their lives, it was not the same. Having a missing loved one is not something you get over. 'As I said before, you get into a bus, train, aeroplane and you look at people's faces, you're looking all the time, it doesn't go away. I get phone calls in the middle of the night. You pick up and you're hoping it might be her, and then you know it isn't, and you start all over again.'

Amelia too said she had been haunted daily ever since her mum vanished. 'I remember five years after Mum went missing, I was working at a hospital in Newcastle. I saw a woman's name on the board, Lorrin Whitehead. My heart dropped. I ran, pushed people out of the way, but it wasn't her. It wasn't Mum.'

Families of missing people have told me time and time again that the feeling doesn't go away. Without a resolution, they cling to hope, which is followed by a disappointment that can be suffocating and debilitating.

While authorities in Lorrin's case still lean towards the theory of suicide, I'm not convinced. What I have learned about Lorrin while investigating her case is that she had an unbreakable and unwavering commitment to her children. She was also making active plans for her future, especially after conquering cancer.

I cannot see her taking her life after winning the battle of her life! And why hasn't her body been found? Remember, she left her house on foot, so she couldn't have gone far, and despite a massive air and ground search, no trace of Lorrin has ever been found. None of it makes sense to me, or to those closest to Lorrin.

'My reason for doubting she could have taken her own life is because she loved those kids so much,' Louise told me. 'I just can't imagine that she would never come back for them.'

Amelia echoed her sentiments. 'She was the happiest I'd seen her in months and months. She just overcame a massive health battle. You know, that's not someone who is going to then go out and suicide.'

From the minute her mum went missing, Amelia has believed that Lorrin was a victim of foul play at the hands of someone she knew. 'I feel that this person is solely responsible for her going missing,' she confided to me. 'And I've confronted them in the past, and, you know, it's really hard because I've actually, over the decade, forgiven them.'

Amelia refused to name the person she believed was responsible for her mum's disappearance. But she did admit they were still a figure in her family's lives.

Her startling admission led me to ask her a difficult question. Did Amelia, after ten years, believe that her mother could still be alive? 'Oh, that's a really hard question,' Amelia replied. 'In all the scenarios in my mind I say no because, as a nurse, I know that she needs her medication for her diabetes, and every six months the police go into the national diabetes registration of Australia and they check if she's accessed insulin and the answer is no. I don't think she's alive anymore, and that really saddens me to say,' Amelia conceded through tears.

It's tough to watch people at their most raw and vulnerable, and it never gets any easier.

Lorrin Whitehead's sudden disappearance was completely out of character, and it came with no warning signs. Her children miss her touch, and they long to hear her voice and to see her comforting smile. No child should grow up without their mum, and Lorrin's kids want answers. Until they get them, their nightmare of not knowing will continue.

'I would never wish it on my worst enemy to have a missing loved one,' Amelia told me, sobbing. 'And that's why we make appeals. I don't particularly like talking about it. I want to live my life, my normal mundane life, but I need to tell the public my mum's story because I want her to be home with me or, if unfortunately she's not alive, I want her remains to come home to us and be laid to rest. I hope I never have to do that. I hope she does come home.'

* * *

In January 2025, police searched bushland and a dam on a property at Dereel, south of Ballarat, Victoria, looking for Lorrin's remains.

Lorrin Whitehead was last seen on Friday, 8 February 2013 at 4.55 pm at a local supermarket in Bannockburn, Victoria. She has not accessed her bank account since and has not made contact with family and friends. There are grave concerns for her welfare, as she is a type-1 insulin-dependent diabetic. According to her family and police, Lorrin's disappearance is completely out of character.

Gordana Kotevski

4

Taken off the Street

Gordana Kotevski

Losing a child is a tragedy no parent should ever have to endure. It's an experience that causes immense pain and suffering, leaving lasting emotional scars. But to lose a child to a violent, senseless act is heartache on a whole other level.

The disappearance of 16-year-old schoolgirl Gordana Kotevski on Thursday, 24 November 1994 has baffled investigators for three decades. I still remember the television news reports and newspaper articles about her vanishing. You don't forget attacks on children.

Gordana went missing at around 9 pm as she was walking to her aunt's house in Newcastle. In my experience, it's unusual for a young girl to be abducted as she walks home. You see it in movies, but it doesn't often happen in real life.

When I started *The Missing Australia* podcast, Gordana's case was one of the first I wanted to cover. However, I knew her family had endured a great deal of disappointment over the years. They'd participated in a lot of media interviews in the hope they would lead to a breakthrough in the case that might finally deliver the answers they so desperately craved. Unfortunately, the case remains unsolved.

When a journalist decides to cover a missing person case, it can be harrowing for the family because they have to publicly revisit the most distressing moment of their lives. This is why it wasn't until two years after I first contacted Gordana's mum, Peggy, and her sister, Carolina, that I proposed we do the story.

We'd spoken many times and had got to know each other to the point where I felt I'd gained their trust. Most importantly, I believed they were strong enough to speak about Gordana.

Peggy Kotevski lives in a modern four-bedroom house in a new estate opposite a lake. As I drove to her home south of Wollongong – which, by coincidence, is where I was born and bred – questions swirled around in my head, questions that I was certain had haunted the Kotevski family for the previous 30 years. The most profound questions were who had taken their loved one, and why?

As an ex-cop turned investigative journalist I take these types of crimes personally because they are an attack on the innocence of society. When I cover a story, I don't just want to repeat what has already been reported in the mainstream media. I want to uncover new information that might lead to breakthroughs that point to the truth.

So as I pulled into the driveway of Peggy's home, I was feeling a profound sense of purpose. This was more than just another interview; it was a step towards justice for Gordana.

Peggy welcomed me warmly with a brave smile, but her eyes betrayed years of pain. I followed her down a long hall to the kitchen and dining area, where she'd laid out banana cake and tea and coffee.

I noticed a small table crowded with family photos, each one a silent testament to happier times. One picture frame in the shape of a love heart caught my eye. Peggy picked up the framed photo and began to speak, her voice steady yet heavy with emotion.

'Gordana was born in 1977. She had dark, dark eyes like her dad and lots of hair. She was very, very small. As she grew older she blossomed into a beautiful young lady,' Peggy said proudly as her fingers stroked the photo frame.

Gordana was born to Peggy and Branco Kotevski. As well as her older sister, Carolina, she had a younger brother, Damian. The Kotevskis were a traditional Macedonian family – strict yet loving, with strong values.

Peggy recalled that, in the week her younger daughter vanished, Gordana was excited to soon be attending her first concert. She was going with her cousin to see the boy band Boyz II Men, and it was to be a significant milestone for her, a taste of freedom she'd never had before.

'I was on afternoon shift,' Peggy recounted, her eyes distant. 'I dropped Gordana off at school, then went to the local shops and bought a little top for her to wear to the concert.'

That was the last time Peggy saw her daughter. Branco picked up the kids from school in the afternoon, and after Damian's indoor soccer game, he dropped Gordana at Charlestown Square shopping centre.

At around 8.45 pm, as the warm summer night descended into darkness, Gordana left the shopping centre on foot. She was heading towards her Aunt Sonia's house, just five minutes away, where she was to be picked up by her mum. But the young girl never made it.

'She was going to walk down, and it was daylight saving so she really thought there was no danger, and the street is pretty safe – not even five minutes from the roundabout up the top from the main road down to Sonia's place,' Peggy explained.

On that fateful night, Gordana's sister, Carolina, had been driving up from Sydney with her husband and newborn baby. I met with Carolina at her place, just a twenty-minute drive from Peggy's.

'When we arrived, I asked Dad, "Where's Gordana?" He said she was out shopping with the girls [and that] Mum was going to pick her up on the way back home [after she finished work],' Carolina recalled. '[Charlestown Square] was our high school hangout on Thursday night. We all used to go there. I used to go there. As I walked past her bedroom I actually thought I saw her lying on her bed. But when I called my aunt at about quarter past nine, she said, "Oh, she's not here" in a weird way. She told me to ring [Gordana's] friends. By the time I did that, my aunt called back and said: "Call the police. We found her wallet and bag on the roadside!" And the nightmare began.'

Gordana's Aunt Sonia had heard screams and sent her husband, Greg, outside to check. But it was too late. The street was empty and Gordana was gone. Greg found

Gordana's wallet and a torn shopping bag on the side of the road, evidence of a violent struggle. The offender must have snatched the shopping bag from Gordana's hand, leaving a partial palm print.

Carolina's voice trembled as she recounted more. 'She was a feisty little bugger. So the bag was from the old Grace Brothers – I think [that's what] the store was called then. It had their grab mark on the bottom of it so they would have dragged her in [to their vehicle] that way. I think it just would have happened all so suddenly. She wouldn't have been expecting it, that's for sure.'

A group of teenagers skateboarding on the same street had heard Gordana's screams and seen a vehicle speed away. Realising a crime had occurred, the skateboarders raced to the police station to report it. They described having seen a light-coloured ute, possibly a Toyota Hilux, driving down the hill earlier and parking on the side of the road. After hearing the screams, they heard two car doors slam, suggesting two people were involved.

Carolina also called Charlestown Police Station. 'When I told them the street name, they said, "You better come to the police station because we've got three witnesses here giving us statements,"' recalled Carolina. 'I didn't know how to tell

Dad. Then we started ringing the hospitals, thinking that maybe someone did something and then tossed her out on the side of the road. It just got worse from there, when we didn't hear anything and there was no ransom. You think somebody would have done it for money.'

Peggy was at work when she got the call. The call that every parent dreads, that changes everything, forever. 'My sister-in-law rang me,' Peggy said, her voice heavy with emotion. 'She said, "I'm coming to get you!"'

When Sonia explained what had happened, Peggy didn't know how to react. 'Everything went through my mind, and the last thing, you know: *Perhaps she's been abducted. Who are these monsters?*'

Peggy's account of that fateful night brought tears to my eyes. When I'm listening to a parent reflect on what can only be described as every parent's worst nightmare, it's hard to disassociate myself. *Who are these monsters?* The weight of Peggy's words hung in the air as a painful reminder of the fragility of life.

I asked Peggy whether she'd understood at that moment that her daughter had been taken.

'The first thing I remember I said was: "Where's the police? Have you notified the police?" At the time, to be honest with you, I was naive. I thought the whole army would go and look for her. That was my expectation because it's a human being we're talking about, and it's someone's child.'

The days that followed were a blur. While police and other emergency services and volunteers were mobilised to search the surrounding bushland for Gordana, the Kostevski family could only sit and wait for what they prayed would be good news. When I spoke to Peggy, I asked her how she had coped. 'I just went blank,' she said. 'I was concerned for Damian and keeping him sort of calm. My husband at the time went ballistic. He was so angry that the police weren't doing more – blocking roads and getting in touch with other resources to help.'

On top of losing their child, Peggy and Branco had to suffer the indignity of being made to feel like persons of interest in Gordana's disappearance. Vicious rumours began to circulate within the tight-knit local Macedonian community. 'Gossip started that I had arranged a marriage for Gordana, and then the police questioned me – had to question me – which was a great insult to my intelligence,' Peggy told me, the tone of her voice changing. 'And they looked into our characters, whether we've done something to her. You know, most of the time they say that families are involved, and I said, "Go right ahead."'

I explained to Peggy that police needed to look first at those who were close to the missing person because they had to eliminate everyone, even family. Peggy shrugged her shoulders in disapproval, and I couldn't blame her, but I also understood that the police had a job to do, and eliminating family members was part of the process.

Carolina spoke of the never-ending questions that had haunted her every day since Gordana vanished. The when, why, who and how. 'It's like a carousel,' she said, her eyes filling with tears. 'It goes around in your mind every single day.'

Peggy and Carolina had shown me photos of the street, but I decided I needed to see the crime scene for myself. I wanted to walk where Gordana was last seen and try to make sense of what they'd told me.

I drove to Newcastle, thinking all the way about what might have happened to Gordana. I pictured the two men inside the truck, waiting in silence for their prey. I couldn't picture their faces but I imagined their eyes, darting around as they made sure no one was there to witness their diabolical crime.

When I reached Charlestown, only about ten minutes south-west of Newcastle's city centre, I took the turnoff onto Charlestown Road, which would lead me to the street where Gordana's Aunt Sonia used to live. Powell Street passes through a section of dense bushland on either side of the road and ends in a residential cul de sac that sends you back the way you came in.

At the top of Powell Street, I parked near a roundabout, got out of the car and began to walk down the hill, just as Gordana did that night. It's a long, steep hill that flattens out momentarily before rising again. Sonia's old house is adjacent to the dip. There are fewer than 20 houses in the street and I didn't notice any street lights. It would have been dark as Gordana walked.

It must have been as she approached the bottom of Powell Street that she was ambushed. It would have taken only seconds – suddenly she was gone and would never be seen again.

I stood on the spot where Gordana was attacked and felt a chill. This sort of indecency shouldn't happen. I surveyed the surroundings. There's thick bushland on both sides, and I pictured local kids exploring and playing games.

Carolina had told me that Gordana had been offered a lift to her aunt's that night but had decided to walk. A sliding-door moment, a fateful decision that changed the lives of so many people. Carolina had painted a vivid picture of the moments leading up to Gordana's disappearance. The casual stroll through familiar streets turning into a nightmare. The torn shopping bag, the discarded wallet and the eerie silence speaking volumes about the horror Gordana endured.

I could see Gordana's aunt's old house from where I was standing. It was so close I could have thrown a tennis ball into the front yard and easily kicked a footy onto the roof. I wanted to know how close Gordana came to reaching her aunt's house, so I began to walk towards the house while counting my steps: 'One, two, three, four … thirty-nine, forty.'

As I walked down Powell Street, the gravity of Gordana's ordeal hit me. That poor girl. She must have been so happy, with a new outfit for her first concert. The last thing on her mind would have been evil lurking in the shadows.

'Forty-one, forty-two, forty-three, forty-four.'

Forty-four steps. The difference between reaching safety and disappearing forever. I stood at the bottom of the driveway, looking at the front door of Sonia's old house, and thought how things could have been so different.

'My sister was the type of girl who would wake me up to go to the toilet at night because she was scared of shadows,' Carolina had told me. 'These things just didn't happen to people like us. We were from a very tight-knit community. My sister would never go out to clubs and parties like girls her age these days. This was a one-off occasion when she decided to walk to my aunt's house.'

Gordana's photo was splashed across the front pages of newspapers around the country, and details of her disappearance filled the nightly television news bulletins for weeks. Hundreds of police on foot, motorbikes and horseback were joined by dozens of volunteers alongside Gordana's family and friends as the surrounding areas were searched, a police chopper hovering above looking for any clues regarding the teenager's disappearance. But despite all the effort, Gordana's case went cold.

***

In 1999, five years after Gordana vanished, Strike Force Fenwick was established to re-examine not only her disappearance but also those of three other missing girls: Leanne Goodall, last seen on Saturday, 30 December 1978 aged 20; Robyn Hickie, who went missing on Saturday, 7 April 1979 aged 18; and 14-year-old Amanda Robinson, who vanished forever on Saturday, 21 April 1979, exactly two weeks after Robyn. Like Gordana, these girls had gone missing from the Newcastle area, leaving a terrible stain on the region's soul, that is still perceptible today.

mcdonald jones stadium
THIS IS
GORDANA
Last seen Charlestown 1994
Call Crime Stoppers
if you have any info
1800 333 000
oh!

I wanted to find out more about the police investigation into Gordana's disappearance, so I asked Peggy and Carolina if they could nominate one of the detectives on the task force who I could try to talk to.

They both pointed to Bill Glen, a retired detective sergeant. Peggy told me Bill had shown her family great compassion and had always kept them up to date with any developments in Gordana's case. But many years had passed and they had lost contact with Bill, and she didn't know where he was living or even if he was still alive.

Luckily, Bill is still alive, and I managed to track him down for an interview. I was eager to learn more about the case and to understand the challenges Bill and the task force faced when they re-investigated Gordana's case years after she disappeared.

Bill now lives in New Zealand, so we talked over Zoom. 'We went back to the beginning. We got all the investigative notes and went through everything,' he explained. 'We had to make a choice at one stage about what vehicle we were going to chase up so we went with Toyota Hilux, but if you see a Nissan Navara next to it, there's not much difference. So we did a review of every Hilux registered in the Newcastle area in 1994. It was a huge task, really, [as] you're finding the vehicles have been sold, or gone interstate, or the owner was dead, or it had been written off in a car accident. We identified everything that had been stolen, and every Hilux in New South Wales was identified.'

The painstaking and tireless efforts of investigators like Bill Glen revealed the magnitude of the task at hand. Tracking every Toyota Hilux in the state was a Herculean effort as there were thousands of cars to trace, but it was a necessary step in piecing together Gordana's final moments. It involved old-fashioned police work, with cops manually and meticulously sifting through files and painstakingly tracing each owner.

Each vehicle represented a potential lead, a thread of hope in the intricate web of circumstances surrounding Gordana Kotevski's disappearance. Bill told me the task force followed up every lead that came in and every suspect who appeared on the police radar.

'We had a situation where a person of interest to us was someone who owned a Hilux and had a record of sexual offences, something like that,' Bill clarified. 'But we were getting hundreds of phone calls like, "If I was you I'd talk to Joe Bloggs, you know, he's a funny-looking bugger and I've always had my suspicions about him." Well, you do a check on [Joe

Bloggs] and he's got no criminal history and there's no record of him ever owning a white ute, so where do you take that?'

Bill said it was necessary to follow every lead, and even whispers of potential suspects had to be pursued so each suspect could be eliminated from the investigation. Some lines of inquiry injected fresh hope into the case, but amidst the glimmers of possibility there were shadows of doubt, and nothing solid was unearthed that led to a breakthrough in Gordana's case.

I remembered reading media reports at the time that suggested Gordana and the other missing girls might have been victims of the same serial killer operating in the Newcastle area. Backpacker serial killer Ivan Milat was, at one time, suspected of being involved, but nothing was ever uncovered to connect him to the disappearances. I asked Bill if he believed Gordana's disappearance was linked to those of the other missing girls.

'I think it was a standalone case,' he said. 'I can only give you a gut feeling, and gut feelings are bad. The only people who should have a gut feeling are police dogs.' He chuckled. 'But I think the time had gone and the people responsible for some of the historical ones would have been well into their 30s. The descriptions of the two people who were in the street are basically late teens, early 20s, so no, I don't think they're connected.'

Bill's gut feeling that Gordana's case stood alone echoed the sentiment of many other investigators. A singular tragedy swirling in a backdrop of uncertainty. The passage of time seemed to distance her fate from those of the other missing girls. It's a theory that is also supported by former New South Wales State Coroner John Abernathy, who presided over the 2003 inquest into Gordana's suspected death. John had never spoken publicly about the case, but I managed to do a short interview with him over the phone in 2023. I started by asking him if he thought the disappearances of Gordana and the other girls were connected.

'In my opinion they weren't,' he said. 'And I came to that view after I looked in detail at all those girls in Newcastle and Gordana Kotevski. Gordana Kotevski, I believe, was a case on its own, even though the body was never found.'

As we've seen, it's the not knowing that destroys the souls of families of missing loved ones. While the Kotevski family have accepted they will never see Gordana alive again, they grieve not having her body to lay to rest. Having your missing loved one returned, even just a piece of them, can have a profound effect.

Even when a missing person is presumed dead, if their remains have not been found, they remain psychologically present, and that leads to family members being preoccupied with the missing person.

The importance of having a body or body part to bury cannot be underestimated. People speak of 'closure'. I prefer the word 'resolution', of which the simple *Britannica Dictionary* definition is 'the act of finding an answer or solution to a conflict, problem, etc'.

No missing person case exemplifies this better than that of 20-year-old Matthew Leveson, who disappeared in 2007. His much older boyfriend, Michael Atkins, stood trial for his murder and manslaughter but was acquitted by a jury in 2009, and Matthew's disappearance remained unexplained.

For years, Matthew's parents, Faye and Mark, spent their weekends driving around bushland in a futile attempt to find their son's grave. They just wanted a body. They, together with police, believed Atkins knew what had happened to Matthew, but he refused to cooperate.

In 2016, however, during a coronial inquest into Matthew's disappearance, Atkins was caught out lying under oath. Facing up to ten years in prison, he was cornered into a deal that gave him immunity from further prosecution for perjury if he gave up where Matthew was buried. Faye and Mark Leveson made a deal with the devil, forced to choose between finding their son and seeking justice. It was an impossible choice but they wanted their son's body back at all costs.

Atkins claimed that Matthew had died of a drug overdose and that Atkins had panicked and disposed of his body by burying it in the Royal National Park, south of Sydney. He drew a map for police and, in 2017, after days of searching and a decade after Matthew was last seen alive, police removed a small palm tree and found his remains.

It must have been a bittersweet moment for Faye and Mark Leveson. Finally, they had their son, and some questions around his disappearance had been answered. However, now the man they believed responsible for his death would never be held accountable.

***

Many families of missing people seek answers in all kinds of places and I don't judge them at all, because I understand the despair they feel in their desperation to find their missing loved one.

Peggy and Carolina Kotevski are also desperate for answers. Together and separately, they have seen numerous psychics and clairvoyants over the years, both in Australia and overseas. In 1996, Peggy even travelled to Bulgaria to see blind psychic Baba Vanga, who is famous for her prophecies coming true. But nothing Baba Vanga told Peggy led to a breakthrough in Gordana's case.

Scepticism often surrounds the use of psychics in missing person cases, but when all else fails, desperate families will try anything, and police have used psychics themselves to try to solve cases.

Carolina told me she and her mum know other people may shake their heads and warn them they are being ripped off and taken advantage of, but they have to try everything to find Gordana. 'It's incredibly important for our own peace of mind, so we can just give her the respect that she deserves as a human being and as the good person that she was.' Carolina paused, her voice soft. '[We need] to lay her to rest. We were robbed of everything from these people, and for all we know, they're still living their life.'

Peggy told me she would do anything to find Gordana. 'There's nothing, whatever you would suggest, whether I believed it or not, I would still do it, till my last breath. You just can't stop.'

'Peggy, would you kill?' I asked her. I expected her to

pause and take a few seconds to think about my question, but she didn't.

'I have said I would,' she fired back immediately with conviction. 'But physically at the moment, I can't do it because I've got arthritis in my trigger-point finger.'

We both laughed before Peggy continued. 'So if I could I would. If I knew who it is I would, and if this country punishes me for it, well, then I feel sad for the whole population. But I would kill.'

If I were in her shoes, I think I would too. Bill Glen said that Gordana's case bears horrifying similarities to one of Australia's worst crimes: the abduction, rape and murder of Sydney nurse Anita Cobby on 2 February 1986. '[The case of] Anita Cobby is probably the only other one like that, you know, a young girl is walking home and she gets dragged into a car. And then there was Gordana.'

When I spoke to Bill he didn't try to hide his contempt for those responsible for snatching Gordana off the street. 'It takes a special kind of animal to behave like that,' he told me. 'I mean, you only have to look at the Cobby killers. They laughed through the whole trial so that describes them and, for this, it's probably someone of the same ilk. There's nothing you could say in their defence; certainly, they have no humanity.' He is long retired from the police force, but Gordana's case is one that he still thinks about, and he hopes with all his heart that it will one day be solved.

While the men who killed Anita Cobby will die in jail, the men who took Gordana are still out there, somewhere. Even when they are caught, Carolina told me nothing will make up for the pain and suffering they inflicted on her family. 'The heartbreaking thing for me to this day is that my poor grandparents passed away and they never found out what happened,' Carolina said. 'They couldn't understand what happened, you know, because you see these things in the movies, it doesn't happen to us. It was very distressing to see my parents and the impact it had on them and their relationship.'

Gordana's parents' marriage was deeply affected by their loss and it didn't survive. Branco lives in another state, and rarely has contact with his ex-wife or children. I have spoken to him over the phone a number of times, most recently after the release of an episode about Gordana on *The Missing Australia* podcast. He is always pleasant. He just wants to discover what I know so that he can find the men who took his daughter. But, unfortunately, I can't help him. If I had information about the perpetrators, I would give it to the police so they could go out and lock them up.

In Branco, I detect an overwhelming sense of loss. He is a man who is broken and wounded, a shell of the man he used to be. He is riddled with guilt. He blames himself for not protecting his little girl. But how could he have known; how could anyone have known?

One thing I do know, however, is that the men who stole Gordana from her family and a life full of promise are cowards. They teamed up to kidnap a teenage girl who barely weighed 40 kilograms. It's sickening even to imagine the fear that poor girl must have felt when she was attacked. I hope they've spent every day of the past 30 years looking over their shoulders. They most probably have families of their own now, and have lived long lives, but one day – and I hope that day comes soon – they'll hear a knock on their door and it will be the police and they will be made to pay for their horrific crime.

In April 2019, Strike Force Arapaima was established to investigate the disappearance and suspected murder of Gordana. Detectives on the task force have confirmed to me that Gordana's case is still an active investigation.

In 2022, the NSW Government increased the reward for information into Gordana's cold case from $100,000 to $1 million. That's a lot of incentive for someone with information to come forward. Gordana's family don't care what that person's motivation may be; they just want them to do the right thing.

So sure, there's a million bucks on offer, but if you know something and you don't come forward, then you're complicit in what happened to that 16-year-old girl.

***

Peggy and Carolina Kotevski are two of the strongest women I have ever met. I've seen many families of missing people crumple under the weight of hopelessness but these women are a powerful force. Their quest for justice has only intensified over the years, and they are determined to find out what happened to their beloved Gordana.

Carolina still sees her sister in her dreams and wishes she could speak to her one more time. 'I would just tell her how much I love her, and how much I've missed her. Yeah, she was my best friend and I do see her in my dreams, sometimes, and it's funny because we never speak to each other but it's like telepathy. I'll fill her in on everything that's been happening and she'll just kiss me on the cheek and hug me and then she'll disappear.'

***

In June 2023, I released an episode of *The Missing Australia* podcast that focused on Gordana's case. As with all stories I investigate, I made an appeal for information and finished with my catchcry: 'Someone, somewhere, knows something.'

Call it an audacious attempt to encourage anyone with information about a missing person case to contact police. Well, a number of people heard my plea and they reached out to Strike Force Arapaima investigators, passing on vital information about Gordana's case that has opened up promising new leads.

One listener to the podcast was triggered by my story on Gordana Kotevski and contacted Strike Force Arapaima about a violent attack she endured back in 1980 when she too was 16 years old. Following an investigation by detectives, the victim was able to identify her attacker, and in January 2024, police arrested a man over the alleged abduction and sexual assault 44 years ago. He was charged with four offences, including abducting a woman with the intention of sexually assaulting her, and assault occasioning actual bodily harm. At the time of writing, the trial has yet to commence.

This huge development gives me hope that Gordana's case will be solved one day soon. All it takes is one person with the courage to look deep into their soul and do the right thing.

Gordana Kotevski and her family deserve that.

5

Baby in the Mail

Baby Doe

Back in the day, when I was a young cop in Sydney's Kings Cross, I quickly learned that there was always someone who knew something that could help solve a crime. The trick was to find them.

That's why, in my podcast, I always include a call to action, in which I try to rally people who may have information about a missing person case to come forward and tell authorities what they know. In a missing person case, that *someone* might be a family member of the person who went missing, or one of their friends. The *something* could be a name, something that was said during a drunken rant or behaviour that raised suspicion.

But what if you had a body and no name? What if it was the person's identity that was missing? Sadly, in the world of missing persons, this isn't uncommon. There are currently more than 700 unidentified bodies lying in morgues and unmarked graves around Australia.

Think about that for a moment. Seven hundred people who no one has tried to find. They are sons and daughters, brothers and sisters, mums and dads, and no one has come forward to claim them.

People without an identity are commonly called John, Jane or Baby Doe, and I believe that every one of them deserves the dignity of having a name. That's why I began to look into a mysterious case that had been baffling police across the Northern Territory and Victoria for 60 years.

In the sweltering heat of a May morning in 1965, the city of Darwin was waking up. Back then, Beatlemania was sweeping the world and Robert Menzies reigned as Australia's prime minister. And amidst the seemingly mundane routines of the day, a rookie cop was about to embark on an investigation that would haunt him for decades.

Denver Marchant was young, fresh-faced and ruggedly handsome. Tall, with an athlete's physique, he'd be conspicuous in a crowd of 50. Denver was keen and eager to prove himself, but when his sergeant called Denver into his office, the young officer had no inkling of the horror that awaited him. The sergeant, a seasoned veteran but weary from years of service, was characteristically brief. 'Ace,' he said, using Denver's nickname, 'there's a job at the Knuckey Street post office. The clerk there needs to speak to the police. Take a car and see what's up.'

Denver assumed it would be a routine call, maybe a break and enter, or a window that some kids had thrown a rock through.

When the young cop arrived at the Knuckey Street post office, it was a hub of activity as customers went about their daily business. However, John Polishak, the clerk who had summoned police, was visibly shaken as he led Denver to the back room.

John pointed at a parcel that lay on a table, partly unwrapped. It was weeping dark fluid, and a smell of decay permeated the air, causing Denver to retch. Trying to maintain his composure, the rookie cop carefully unwrapped the package. Inside he found a tiny lifeless body, that of a baby boy, unclothed and still attached to his umbilical cord.

'I'd never seen anything like it in my life,' Denver recalled when I spoke to him in 2023, shock still echoing in his voice. 'The child was quite decomposed, and the thing that struck me immediately was a ligature around the neck that was cut off. It was ascertained to be a stocking.'

Denver said the sight was ghastly. The baby appeared to have been brutally murdered just minutes after he was born, then his tiny body discarded like garbage.

'John was in a state of shock, which is probably a mild way of putting it. He was really shaken up and he said this parcel had been there for about eight days.'

After being killed, the baby had been wrapped in newspaper before being stuffed inside a postal package with six penny stamps affixed to it. It was mailed from the Russell Street Postal Building in Melbourne to the Knuckey Street post office in Darwin on 3 May 1965.

The address on the parcel read 'J Anderson, Darwin'. However, no one by that name had come forward to claim it. The return address – 'JF Barnes, 2 Woolridge Avenue, Mentone, Victoria' – did not exist.

Back in 1965, uniformed police handled pretty much everything, including forensics, so Denver took photos of the scene and arranged for the body to be taken to the local mortuary. Back then, Darwin's morgue was a small, un-airconditioned facility with only a few fridges. The baby was placed inside a fridge to await a post-mortem examination.

Denver Marchant

'I was told a few days later there was to be a post-mortem and to attend. I'm fairly sure Dr Hunter undertook the post-mortem. I don't know how many post-mortems I've been to but it's hundreds and hundreds. But I'd never seen anything like this in my life,' Denver said. 'The child was quite decomposed, so much so that the doctor undertook the post-mortem with just a large pair of scissors.'

Denver remembered that Dr Hunter, a tall, thin man with a kind demeanour, was physically sick during the post-mortem. At its conclusion it was established that the stocking had been wrapped four times around the child's neck. But the most chilling revelation came when Dr Hunter confirmed that the baby had taken a breath before his death.

This was no stillbirth; it was cold-blooded murder. The baby's life had been snuffed out immediately on entering the world.

From the outset, Denver's investigation faced numerous obstacles. In 1965, police work was labour-intensive. Without computers, every search required sifting through physical records, which was time-consuming. Making the job even harder was the fact that Anderson was a common name. And what did the initial J stand for? Was it John, Jeff, James?

Trying to identify 'J Anderson' in a transient population like Darwin's was nearly impossible.

Police were also unable to extract fingerprints from the package, and of course this was many years before DNA was discovered. With no leads, the task of identifying the killer seemed insurmountable.

From the beginning, Denver speculated about the identity of the killer. The brutal nature of the crime suggested deep malice. He couldn't imagine a woman committing such an act, but postnatal mental illness could not be ruled out.

'I just can't imagine a woman doing that to a child and then posting the child away. It just seems illogical, unless, of course, you've got a mental capacity which is just pure hatred,' Denver surmised.

Perhaps she had been abandoned by the father of the baby. Or perhaps she had become pregnant out of wedlock and her adultery had only become clear to her enraged husband after the baby's birth.

Inquiries by police in Victoria led them to believe a man had posted the package, but the description of the man was vague, and with no CCTV around back then, the lead proved tenuous.

The baby was buried in a Darwin cemetery, but the murder had occurred in Victoria, so the case fell under the jurisdiction of Victoria Police. With no statute of limitations on murder, the hunt for the killer continued.

As the years passed, the story of the baby in the mail remained one of Australia's most brutal and macabre mysteries, although it wasn't well known.

I first heard about it in 2017 from a detective who was in charge of the Northern Territory missing persons unit. The case both fascinated and unnerved me, and I was determined to do whatever I could to try to give this baby a proper name.

So, in 2023, I began working on the case. My first priority was to find out if Denver was still alive. Luckily, he was. I tracked him down in Hervey Bay, Queensland, and flew up to interview him.

Denver picked me up at the airport. At 83 years old, he was still an imposing figure, with a lean body and gravelly voice that demanded your attention. We drove to a local park and sat down at a picnic table, where he told me the story.

His voice carried the weight of years of unresolved grief and frustration. From a plastic A4 folder he produced black-and-white photos he'd taken of the grotesque package. Although the body was badly decomposed, I could clearly tell that the baby was a newborn, with a healthy head of hair.

Most retired cops have one unsolved case that sticks with them long after they leave the police, and for Denver, the image of the tiny lifeless body was something he had never been able to erase from his mind.

He picked up one of the photos and stared at it before turning to me. 'I don't know how many deaths I've been to,' he said. 'I couldn't count, I've been to so many. It's just a bizarre thing to actually post a child in the mail. I don't think there's any case in Australia like it, and it's something that just really sticks with you.'

Denver said he sometimes wished he had a delete button to get the image inside the post office out of his head, but he couldn't. It stayed with him.

He was candid about the fact that he might not have many years left to see the mystery resolved. 'Before I shuffle off and hit the furnace, I'd like to see something positive come out of this,' he told me.

He'd been interviewed about the case countless times over the years, but had never admitted that he harboured a theory about who the mysterious J Anderson could be. Sixty years after he walked into the Knuckey Street post office in Darwin as a young constable, Denver revealed to me who he suspected the baby's father might have been.

'There was one J Anderson, and I actually knew him in Darwin,' Denver said. 'He was a fine fellow, a wonderful sportsman and a friend. Jim and I got along quite well, but as far as sporting attributes are concerned, he was a long way out of my league. Put it this way, he was fast and I was slow,' he said with a chuckle.

Denver's suspicions were based on Jim Anderson's reputation with women, but he had never been able to prove anything. Delving into someone's private life, especially without a shred of evidence, was a delicate matter, particularly for a junior constable. Senior detectives had been tasked with trying to identify the mysterious J Anderson, and Denver, respecting the hierarchy, had stepped back.

'I didn't really broach the subject with him. There was no offence, no offence in the Northern Territory, so it can be shaky ground talking to someone about things like that. There's absolutely nothing he's done wrong, if just merely an association with the child.'

Of course, Denver was right. Sleeping with someone and getting them pregnant is not an offence.

I asked Denver to tell me more about Jim Anderson. He told me that Jim was now deceased, but he believed his children were still alive and possibly living in Darwin. If Jim

Anderson was the father, his children could provide DNA to compare with the baby's DNA, which just might lead to the child's killer.

'That's the main thing, the main thrust, to find out who murdered the child,' Denver said emphatically. 'It's a Victorian case; Victoria has carriage of it. There's been no offences committed in the Northern Territory by anyone connected to that child. If the Victorians can get a result, it would be wonderful to see.'

As Denver recounted his long-held theory, I could tell that the unresolved cold case still weighed heavily on him. Like me, he was desperate for a result.

After speaking to Denver, I returned to Sydney, energised by the feeling that we were a step closer to solving the case. I contacted the Northern Territory Police Force and learned that in 2022 they had applied to Deputy Coroner Kelvin Currie to exhume the baby's body, but he had declined the application.

I contacted Mr Currie to find out the reasons behind his decision and he wrote back saying more information was required. 'It will be up to investigating authorities to provide reasons that are sufficient for a coroner to reasonably believe that it is necessary for an investigation, as per section 24 of the *Coroner's Act*,' Mr Currie wrote.

I completely understood what he meant. While the key to unlocking this cold case lay with the child's DNA, the path to acquiring such crucial evidence was fraught with emotional and ethical challenges.

I suspected that Mr Currie wanted more information about the likelihood of being able to extract a DNA sample from a body that was 60 years old, but in recent years scientists in Spain had extracted DNA from a 430,000-year-old Neanderthal's fossilised tooth and thigh bone. Sixty years seemed inconsequential by comparison.

In 2018, the capture of the Golden State Killer in the United States showed the power of DNA technology. Joseph James DeAngelo, a former policeman, was identified and arrested after decades of eluding authorities, thanks to DNA evidence recovered from crime scenes and matched to an online genealogy database.

So, armed with the biggest development in the case in 60 years, I featured the story of the baby in the mail in a new series of *The Missing Australia* podcast, revealing for the first time that the mysterious J Anderson to whom the package was addressed could be local sporting icon Jimmy Anderson.

Before releasing the episode, I felt it was vital that I let Jim Anderson's surviving children and family know of the possible connection between their dad and the baby. I managed to track down one of Jim's grandsons who, like his grandfather, was a successful sportsman in a high-profile sports team. I spoke to the club's media manager, explaining the situation, and he assured me he would pass on the message and tell Jim's grandson to let the rest of the family know about the bombshell new development.

When the episode was released, something remarkable happened. A message arrived from the vast, remote Kimberley region of far north Australia. Jimmy Anderson's daughter Amelia reached out, bringing a glimmer of hope to the cold case.

Although I'd tried to inform the family about the upcoming story, Amelia's nephew had failed to let her know, so the shock was still sinking in. Now that Amelia had heard the story, she felt compelled to make contact. Mention of her father's initial and family name, J Anderson, as well as the timeline of events, had sent chills down her spine. She had to know more.

Amelia's message was a potential breakthrough. She and I connected over a Zoom call one Friday night and her voice shook as she recalled her family history. While her father, Jimmy, had been a renowned sportsman and a legend in the

Northern Territory, he had also been a man known for his infidelity.

'Just to see my dad's initials, to see his name. I was instantly distressed, confused. Growing up, we never heard any rumours about this. And now, hearing this story, it was overwhelming.'

Amelia described how her mother had three children with Jimmy by the age of 15. Despite Jimmy's unfaithfulness, her mother stayed with him, enduring much for the sake of their family.

'Mum had three children at that time in 1965, and they would have all been little. Dad was very much a ladies' man. My mother did put up with a lot from him,' Amelia said. 'We've overcome the shock of it now, so we just want to see if we can give bubba some closure. That could have been our big brother. My instinct says that's my big brother. As soon as I saw the name I got goosebumps, you know, in my heart. You know you get that feeling in your belly? I just knew, I just know he's my big brother. We want to give him a name, a headstone, and the love he never had.'

Amelia's conviction, supported by her belief that her family was the only Anderson family in Darwin at the time, seemed to add weight to the theory that the parcel was indeed meant for her father. 'I've never heard about this case in all my life,' she told me. 'I'm 53 years old, and to hear a story about a cold case that's 60 years old, and it could have a connection to my father, well, I want closure for that detective who's been on the case for so long, and also for that little baby. That little baby needs closure too.'

'Are you prepared to give DNA?' I asked Amelia.

'Yes, definitely,' she replied without hesitation.

A couple of days after we spoke, Amelia was contacted by the Northern Territory Police, who arranged for her to go to Darwin and attend the police station. There, officers took a DNA sample from her.

With the discovery of a possible relative of the baby, Detective Senior Constable Glen Chatto of the Northern Territory Cold Case Task Force again sought permission from the Deputy Coroner to exhume the baby's body, hoping modern forensics could finally unveil his identity, and perhaps that of his killer.

This time the application was successful, and on 22 November 2023, dozens of police, including detectives from the Cold Case Task Force, and council workers with excavators descended on the Darwin General Cemetery in Jingili to dig up a baby buried decades earlier.

By the time we arrived at 8.30 am, barriers had been erected around the gravesite to shield the public from the grim task ahead. The sound of the excavator pierced the morning air and shook the ground.

I began to wonder how deep they would have to dig before they reached the coffin, and whether the baby had been buried in a simple pine box or something more substantial. But no, I thought to myself, the reality was that, as a child who had no known family, he would have received a pauper's funeral funded by the public purse.

Detective Chatto watched on, acutely aware of the significance of what was unfolding. 'This has been on the radar since 1965, so it's been an ongoing investigation since then,' he told me.

Two hours after the excavator roared to life it fell silent. Two men appeared from behind the barricade, pushing a gurney draped in a dark vinyl blanket. They carefully wheeled it to a waiting van. A small lump was visible under the cover, symbolising both tragedy and hope, perhaps the first step in giving the baby a name and seeking justice.

Detective Chatto said the baby would be kept at the morgue, where forensic experts would try to extract a viable DNA sample from his tiny body. The plan was to compare the baby's DNA with Amelia's to see if there was a paternal link establishing Jimmy Anderson as the baby's father.

'Back in the day, there was no such thing as DNA. Now we've got the technology to deal with it, or to progress a case, but it's still a long, drawn-out process,' Detective Chatto said. 'This is an ongoing investigation. We're committed to finding answers no matter how long it takes.'

It didn't take long to get an answer to one of the biggest questions surrounding this case. Two months after the baby's body was exhumed, Amelia rang me with news. 'Jimmy's not the father,' she said bluntly. 'The baby's not our big brother. The DNA is not a match.'

I could hear both disappointment and relief in Amelia's voice. She was relieved because a scandal within her family had been avoided, but she was disappointed that now there was no relationship established between her family and the baby, so she didn't have a legal or moral right to arrange a proper burial and give him a name.

I also felt a little downcast, because Denver's theory had been proven wrong and we had hit another dead end. However, I quickly realised that getting the baby's DNA was a significant step towards discovering what had happened back in May 1965.

DNA is a powerful investigative tool and it presented a new starting point for police in a case that had remained unsolved for 60 years. Using DNA to trace long-lost families or to build your family tree has become extremely popular around the world, with millions of people using various companies that provide the service.

Northern Territory Police would now be able to compare the baby in the mail's DNA with different samples on numerous DNA databases in the hope of getting a match that might take them another step closer to identifying the baby's mother and father.

The forgotten parcel sent from Melbourne to Darwin may finally reveal its secrets, bringing justice and closure to a case that was long overshadowed by intrigue and silence.

And a retired ex-cop may finally get to resolve the one case that has eluded him.

STATE-WIDE HUNT FOR MISSING GIRL

The two-week long search for a missing 15-year-old Kingswood girl has been extended to all parts of the State.

The girl, Lynette Ann Melbin, was last seen in Penrith Plaza on June 5.

Penrith detectives had issued a photograph and description to all metropolitan and country police stations, Det. Sgt. K. Sawyer, said on Monday.

All policewomen had been asked to keep an eye out for the missing girl, he said.

Lynette is five feet one inch tall, and of medium build.

She has fair complexion and long shoulder-length fair to blond hair.

When last seen she was wearing a silver wristlet watch with a black band.

On her right hand she had two friendship rings.

A signet ring was worn on the left hand.

Lynette was also wearing a gold cross on a chain around her neck.

Sgt. Sawyer said that when last seen Lynette had been wearing blue jeans, a short sleeved cream cardigan and blue gym shoes.

"We fear greatly for her safety," Sgt. Sawyer said.

"Her family, and particularly her twin sister, are most distressed."

Anyone knowing the whereabouts of Lynette should contact the nearest police station or Sgt. Sawyer at Penrith 2 [illegible].

A snapshot taken of Lynette Melbin recently.

POLICE BOOKED 399 MOTORISTS

A total of [illegible] offenders were booked by members of No. [illegible] police division during the Queen's Holiday weekend.

Officer in charge Penrith Traffic Office, Sgt. R. [illegible], said all had been booked under the Motor Traffic Act.

Ten people had been booked for traffic offences.

[illegible]or has a majority

[illegible] two new aldermen on Saturday [illegible] majority in Blacktown Council.

A total of [illegible]

Lynette's disappearance was first covered in *The Daily Mirror* in June 1972.

6

My Missing Half

Lynette Melbin

On Monday, 5 June 1972, 15-year-old schoolgirl Lynette Melbin disappeared from Penrith in greater western Sydney. Back then, Penrith was a quiet town, the kind of place where everyone knew everyone. But when Lynette disappeared, the sense of safety in this small community vanished. In that instant, the lives of her parents, Terry and Pam, her twin sister, Liana, her younger sister, Debra, and brother, Terry, were irrevocably shattered. Their lives changed forever, as they were left to grapple with the unknown.

Lynette's mother recounted the events of that dreadful day to me with a voice full of sorrow and pain. 'She came into

Woolworths where I was working,' she recalled. 'She asked if she could go to her boyfriend's place. I said yes and told her I'd pick her up at 4.30 pm when I finished work. But when I got there, she wasn't there.'

Pam's husband, Terry, told me the disappearance of their daughter had left an open wound that had never healed. 'Then you go to the Coroner's Court and you hear them say that somewhere on or around the fifth of June 1972 our daughter met her death, and that's hard to take all these years.'

More than 50 years have passed since Lynette vanished, and yet for the Melbin family the wound is as fresh as ever. They had never given up searching for Lynette, but as time passed, their hope had faded – until the dogged determination of an ex-cop rekindled it.

Neville Scullion was a former NSW Police detective whom I had known for more than 30 years. We'd worked together as detectives in the chaotic precincts of Darlinghurst and Kings Cross during the 1980s and early 1990s. We were younger then, with the confidence that comes with youth and a badge. Times had changed since then and we had both been out of the police a long time, but Neville was drawn into Lynette's case through a personal connection.

'I've been involved in go-karting for a number of years,' he explained as we drove to Penrith from his home in the Sutherland Shire. 'Through go-karting I met a fellow named Tracy Stewart. Tracy's wife, Liana, is the twin sister of Lynette Melbin.'

Liana and her family felt the case of their missing loved one had been forgotten, so when they reached out to Neville, he couldn't turn them down. 'You feel the grief that's been suffered by the family,' he told me, his voice full of empathy. 'You just want to help them. Do your best, use whatever skills you've got to help them get closure.'

When Neville contacted me around 2019 and asked for my help on the case, I too couldn't say no. The case intrigued me and I wanted to help my friend, but there was another reason why I couldn't turn Neville down: Liana was part of the police family. She'd been married to a NSW Police officer named Peter Addison who, along with his workmate Robert Spears, had been murdered by a gunman after responding to a domestic violence call in Crescent Head on the Mid North Coast of New South Wales on 9 July 1995. Liana and her family had suffered unimaginable grief, as had the family of Robert Spears, so there was no way I could ignore her appeal for help.

Neville had thrown himself into the case and spent months piecing together the fragments of the day more than 50 years ago when Lynette disappeared. He'd managed to track down the original detective in charge of the case, had found and interviewed new witnesses and had reviewed the coroner's inquest report. The more Neville dug, the more he became convinced that Lynette had been abducted and murdered by a local man called John Flitcroft.

Flitcroft's name had lingered in the shadows of the investigation, but no bona fide connection was ever established between him and Lynette's disappearance. Flitcroft was a grocery delivery driver back in 1972, a familiar face in the small Penrith community. During his inquiries, Neville had found a witness who had been a young boy at the time, who had seen Lynette talking to a man with a panel van or similar type of vehicle on the day she disappeared.

'They'd seen Lynette talking to a male person with a panel van,' Neville said. 'Now we've established that John Flitcroft either owned or had use of a panel van around that time because he was doing the grocery delivery run with the supermarket.' This was the same supermarket where Lynette's mum worked.

It was an important lead that unfortunately had slipped through the cracks during the initial police investigation, due to the fact that this critical eyewitness had not come forward.

'He was only 15 at the time,' Neville explained. 'He was asked why he never told the police about it, and he thought that the police would just be all over that at the time of the disappearance. Being a 15-year-old kid, he didn't know too much better, I guess.'

It was a tragic oversight, one that might have allowed Flitcroft to evade the initial police net. As Neville continued to dig into Flitcroft's past, he uncovered a disturbing pattern of behaviour and a predilection for young girls like Lynette. 'His first marriage was to a girl who was his neighbour,' Neville told me. 'She was only 16 at the time. The son he had with her grew up and got married, but within two weeks of him being married, his wife left him and took up with his father, John Flitcroft. So it would seem that he had a fetish for young girls.'

Flitcroft's obsession with young girls was likely predatory in nature, in which case he fitted the profile of someone who would target and harm Lynette.

Neville also tracked down Flitcroft's ex-wife, and what she told him sent shivers down his spine. '[She] indicated that she finally left John Flitcroft when she was involved in an argument with him, and she says that he put a cloth over her mouth, which she believed might have had chloroform or a similar sort of substance, to try and render her unconscious.'

An obsession with young girls and a violent streak. I wondered whether the incident with Flitcroft's former wife had been a dress rehearsal for what was to come later.

On the day Lynette disappeared, she had been hanging out at Penrith Plaza with some of her friends. She spoke to her mum at the supermarket and told her she was going to catch the bus home to get changed, and then walk to her boyfriend's house. But she never made it to her boyfriend's house.

Neville said that the original investigators spoke to the bus driver, who was adamant that he didn't see Lynette. 'So that indicates that she never got on the bus to go home,' Neville said, 'but her mother said she definitely got home because the clothes that she was wearing were in the bedroom. So she changed clothes and put on a maroon top and some sort of pants when she left the place.'

Someone gave Lynette a lift home from the shops that day, but who? Remember, Flitcroft was a delivery driver for the supermarket that Lynette's mum worked for, so there is every chance the teenager would have seen Flitcroft there and maybe even met him. Did she accept a ride from Flitcroft, who took her to her home, where she went inside and got changed, after which she got back into his car, expecting that he would drop her off at her boyfriend's? Was it possible that, instead, Flitcroft abducted Lynette and murdered her?

The more Neville uncovered, the more I became convinced that he was on the right track. I then discovered that in 2010 police reviewing Lynette's case had travelled to Adelaide, where Flitcroft was living, to interview him. When detectives spoke to Flitcroft, he was very sick and dying of brain cancer. Police said he denied any involvement in Lynette's disappearance, but one of the detectives who spoke to him admitted to me later that they left the interview convinced that Flitcroft was somehow involved in Lynette's disappearance. And while Flitcroft made no admissions, I believe he slipped up during the interview by admitting to police that he knew the Melbin family and that he had been inside the family home.

I asked Pam Melbin whether she knew Flitcroft but she vehemently denied it, and also absolutely denied that he had been in her home. 'No,' she said, her voice firm. 'He was never inside my house. I would remember.'

So why would Flitcroft admit to being inside the Melbin family home? Well, I think he did so to cover his tracks. I believe he feared that police had possibly uncovered his DNA from the house all those years later. By telling police he knew Pam and had been inside the Melbin house, he was trying to explain away the presence of his DNA, if police had found it. But the crime occurred a long time before DNA was even considered as a tool for law enforcement. If I'm right, it shows not only how conniving Flitcroft was but also that he had a guilty conscience.

Flitcroft died in 2010, so the truth about what had happened to Lynette seemed destined to remain unknown forever. But Neville wasn't ready to give up. He and Lynette's twin sister, Liana, turned to renowned psychic Debbie Malone in a last-ditch effort to find Lynette's remains.

Yes, there have been cases of unscrupulous clairvoyants who have taken advantage of vulnerable people, but Debbie Malone had a solid reputation for accuracy, and the Melbin family were willing to grasp at any straw that might lead them to Lynette.

After a session with Liana, Debbie pinpointed a location, Tench Reserve, a park alongside the Nepean River in Penrith. She believed this was where Lynette had been buried all those years ago. The park is a popular place now where families picnic. But back in 1972, it was an isolated stretch of bushland, the kind of place where you could hide something or someone, and it was just a few kilometres from where Flitcroft lived, which was just around the corner from Lynette's then boyfriend.

On a sweltering Sydney summer day in January 2020, Neville and I drove out to Tench Reserve, where we had arranged to meet Liana and her family, to search the area for Lynette's grave. As we drove out of the suburbs and onto the freeway, I could feel the weight of the past 50 years. Echoing in my mind were Liana's words to me in a phone call a few days before. '[I] always, always think about it. She is my biggest loss. Not having that person beside you, it's just horrible. Everything would be different if she was still here. Our whole life changed that day.'

For Neville, who had invested so much time and effort in reinvestigating the case, it had become personal. He wasn't just an acquaintance – he had come to know and like the Melbin family over the years, and had become close to them, so he felt their grief as if it were his own. 'Having her missing, it's been dreadful for the family,' he said. 'The emotions are just too hard to describe. Where there's a missing family relative involved, it's imperative that they try and find closure. The only way they can find closure in this matter is to find and locate the remains of Lynette. At least then the family can have a proper burial and know what happened to her.'

I knew all too well how important it was that a family get some form of resolution, so I'd pulled out all stops to help the Melbin family, organising for Julie Cowan, a cadaver dog handler from Victoria, to meet us at Tench Reserve to help with the search. Despite having travelled hundreds of kilometres, Julie wasn't charging us a cent for her assistance.

Cadaver dogs are extraordinary. With a sense of smell 40 times greater than a human's, they can detect scents hidden underground, in water and even in the air. Julie's dog Rayne could detect human remains more than 40 years old, and Julie and her team had assisted Victoria Police in numerous searches over many years, so she was an expert in finding hidden dead bodies. On top of that, I had found Julie through an old police colleague of mine, a man named Dave Wright, who had been a police dog handler for more than 20 years. Dave had retired from the NSW Police Force and started up a private company training dogs for the military and police forces around the world. He had trained Julie and her dog, so I knew they were very well qualified.

After about an hour in the car, Neville and I pulled up at Tench Reserve, where children's laughter could be heard above the chirping of rainbow lorikeets. Julie was already there and we exchanged warm greetings before Neville and

I briefed her on what the psychic Debbie Malone had seen. Debbie had said that Lynette was frightened and struggling in a car with her killer. 'She said he drove here, dragged her body and hid it in the bushes, where he covered it in a green sheet,' I told Julie. 'And then he came back later that night to bury her.' The details were chilling, but they gave us a starting point.

As Julie, Neville and I prepared to begin the search, the Melbin family stood nearby, their faces a mix of apprehension and hope that only those with a lost loved one could understand. Terry and Pam were seated on a bench holding hands. Standing beside them were Liana and her husband, Tracy, who had wrapped his arms around his wife like a comforting blanket.

In preparation for the search that day, Neville had gone to the local council and found records describing Tench Reserve back in 1972. He told us the area had changed a lot over the years. Landfill had been dumped, vegetation had become overgrown, and a walking path and road had been built, so it looked nothing like it had back when Lynette vanished. Still, we had to try.

I looked at Lynette's family, huddled together on the high side of the reserve, and tried to imagine how they were feeling as they stared over a grassy embankment that might conceal

Lynette's remains. I noticed tears in Liana's eyes, which she wiped away with a tissue. Pam's eyes, too, were filled with tears. Terry squeezed her hand a little tighter and moved in to whisper something in her ear. I was sure it was something reassuring, like many things he had told her over 50 years, to keep even the faintest glimmer of hope alive.

I wanted to go over to them and say something to make them all feel better, but I didn't know what. I couldn't think of any adequate words at such a sombre time, so I said nothing.

As Julie and Rayne began their search, the air was rife with anticipation. We watched in silence, our eyes darting and following the dog's every move. I could feel tension in my chest: the hope that had brought us all there that day and the fear that we might leave empty-handed.

Rayne sniffed the ground, his tail wagging as he picked up scents, his nose touching and hovering over the ground. Julie watched him intently, looking for signs and ready to reward him if he found something. Then the stifling heat and native birds started to distract him, so Julie gave Rayne a short break to refocus.

I took this opportunity to walk over to Liana and ask her some questions. I began by asking her how important it would be for her parents, who were now in their 80s, to find Lynette

Liana and Lynette Melbin

while they were still alive. 'It is the most important thing in their lives,' she said, tears welling again in her eyes. 'There is nothing more they need in their life than to be able to bury her. Years ago, Tracy got me this beautiful memorial rock and I put a poem there, and when my parents would come and visit they would actually go and put roses on the memorial rock. So for them to have a place to go would just be incredible, before something bad happens and they're not here.'

After a quick break Rayne returned to work. 'Good boy, find it, find it … yeah, good boy,' Julie yelled to encourage him. Rayne led Julie to a spot off a walking track at the base of a stone retaining wall. Four times he sat down, indicating that he had found something. Each time, Julie walked him away then let him run free, and each time he returned to the exact same spot.

Julie came over to where we were all waiting. As she spoke to us, her voice was steady, filled with a mixture of excitement and dread. She pointed towards the track. 'When I brought him down this way he showed a lot of interest along this wall face,' she said. 'And the only thing that he could have found is human remains.'

I felt a chill down my spine. Could this really be it? Had we finally found Lynette after half a century?

The area had now become a potential crime scene so I phoned a friend at the NSW Police Homicide Squad. He arranged for local detectives to come and see us at Tench Reserve. They arrived in less than an hour – one male and two female officers.

Neville filled them in on what we were doing and what we had potentially discovered. The cops gave no indication of what they were thinking. However, they got on the phone and arranged for the NSW Police Dog Unit to come and search the area the next day.

We were all excited that something was being done, but the following day the police dog failed to pick up anything. It was an anti-climax, but we weren't surprised. The police dog, unlike Rayne, was not trained to detect human remains up to 40 years old, so I guess you could say it had been a wasted exercise.

Despite the letdown, Neville and I, and especially Lynette's family, weren't ready to close the book on the case. Julie's dog had signalled something and we couldn't just walk away. We needed to look into it more deeply, which meant digging up the area. The Melbin family agreed, so a few days later we returned.

Neville and I brought reinforcements, namely another ex-cop named Bob Gibbs, who was a former NSW Police crime scene expert. He'd spent 30 years in the police, 21 of them in the scientific squad, forensically gathering and examining evidence from crime scenes. Bob's expertise would ensure that we followed the correct protocols in our search for Lynette's remains.

Bob came equipped with tools for the work ahead. They were implements that were similar to those used by archaeologists: small hand shovels, spades, buckets, a flat trowel and a mattock. He also had a writing pad and pen to record anything we found, and he had brought a camera to take photographs, to record everything in situ, which in simple terms means to have records of the scene before, during and after the excavation.

Neville and I helped Bob grab his tools from the back of his car then walked down to the area where Rayne had shown interest. 'See these two trees? You can see just in front of them the land has been disturbed. It's where the cadaver dog was, and he dropped on the spot, and then Julie removed a bit of undergrowth and then the dog went back three more times,' Neville stressed.

'Good spot to dispose of a body, I guess,' Bob replied, deadpan.

Before beginning, Bob took photos of the area to provide a

permanent record of how it appeared before we started. Then he began to dig. Every shovelful of earth potentially brought us closer to Lynette. The digging was necessarily slow and methodical. Bob was meticulous, ensuring we didn't disturb any potential evidence.

'This dog allegedly can tell the difference between human remains and animals?' Bob asked with cynicism in his voice.

'The dog's trained only to detect human remains up to 40 years,' Neville shot back.

I detected a sliver of scepticism in Bob's question but I understood it and I welcomed it. As a former forensic officer, Bob could not afford to make mistakes. He had to be painstaking when searching for and gathering vital evidence because it would be presented to a court and might determine someone's guilt or innocence. 'I'm the world's biggest sceptic, but I believe the dog,' Bob said, offering a glimmer of hope amidst our growing doubts.

Neville and I each picked up a tool and began to help Bob dig. The ground was hard and stubborn, resisting our efforts as we slowly peeled back layers of earth, trying to uncover any secrets buried below.

We struck something hard. 'It's just a piece of concrete,' I muttered.

Bob grabbed the mallet and began to break it up, shoving the pieces to the side. 'You probably know from your experience, Meni,' Bob said, 'criminals are really lazy. That's why they become criminals. I've maybe done ten burials that were all fairly shallow, apart from one, which was Robert Rose, the serial killer. He buried a body in the Marramarra National Park and that was down about 3 metres, but he had sandy soil.'

I was enjoying having Bob there. He had a million stories to tell, and hearing them was breaking up the monotony of the digging. We kept going, hitting dead ends. More garbage, such as a chip packet with an expiry date long after Lynette disappeared. We removed bricks, roof tiles and twisted pieces of metal. It was clear the reserve had been a dumping ground for years.

The hours stretched on, with Bob sharing more stories to lighten the mood. He told us of a murder in Narrabeen on Sydney's northern beaches, where he'd been lucky enough to find the body within minutes. 'I just pushed the shovel in, and there he was,' he said.

But luck wasn't on our side that day. As the hours dragged on into the afternoon, exhaustion set in. We'd been at it since early morning, digging through layers of topsoil, only to hit rock-hard subsoil that stopped our progress.

Liana and Tracy had been there all day too. Sensing our frustration, Tracy called in a favour from a mate who owned a small excavator, hoping it would speed things up.

Tracy's mate turned up within half an hour and immediately got stuck in. The machine ploughed through the ground with ease, turning up more rubbish. 'A goon bag,' Neville remarked, referring to the bladder of a wine cask. Within minutes the excavator had made a massive hole more than 2 metres deep, but there was no sign of human remains.

'How are you feeling?' I asked Neville quietly.

'I'm gutted,' he said, voicing how we all felt. 'I honestly believed that with all the information we had, the dog, everything, we would have found something.' Neville's voice was heavy with disappointment, his face weary.

Standing by the gaping hole we'd created, I also felt a profound disappointment. I'm always positive that I'll find something to help solve a missing person case, always. If I didn't believe I would, then what would be the point of trying?

We all felt the weight of failure. You raise your hopes and pray that you're on the right track, only to walk away empty-handed.

We packed up the gear, watched as the excavator refilled the hole, then walked away, wondering whether we should have kept digging. We had tried our best but we'd failed to discover any clues.

I looked over at Liana. Her eyes expressed a similar sorrow to Neville's and mine. The hope that had briefly lifted her spirits a week earlier was again fading, replaced by the relentless pain of unanswered questions.

We hugged and I apologised to Liana and Tracy. They both assured me I had nothing to be sorry for and thanked Neville, Bob and me for our efforts. We promised Liana and her family that we'd continue to do whatever we could to help find Lynette.

'I think the family's going to be devastated,' Neville said softly as he and I walked back to his car. 'They held high hopes that they were going to find the remains of their missing daughter and sibling and, unfortunately, that hasn't happened. Unfortunately, we excavated around where the dog had indicated there may be human remains but we haven't managed to find anything.'

As we drove away from Tench Reserve, the evening sky now painted in strokes of orange and pink, I couldn't help but think of Lynette and the life she should have lived; of Liana, who had spent 50 years yearning and searching for her other half; and of Pam and Terry, who had suffered the greatest loss any human can suffer: losing a child.

***

While researching Lynette Melbin's case, we managed to find the newspaper article from June 1972 that first reported her disappearance. A local Penrith man had kept it all these years, then came across it when he cleaned out his shed.

> **Statewide hunt for missing girl**
>
> The two-week–long search for a missing 15-year-old Kingswood girl has been expanded to all parts of the state. The girl, Lynette Ann Melbin, was last seen at Penrith Plaza on June 5. Penrith detectives had issued a photograph and description to all metropolitan and country police stations, Detective Sgt K Sawyer said on Monday. All police women had been asked to keep an eye out for the missing girl, he said. Lynette is five feet one inch tall, and of medium build. She has a fair complexion, and long shoulder-length fair to blonde hair.

Sadly, Pamela Melbin died without knowing what happened to her daughter Lynette. She passed away on 20 July 2020, just months after we conducted our search. Her husband, Terry, who is now 88 years old, clings to the eternal hope that he will find Lynette and bring her home before he too leaves this world.

We have passed on all the information we have discovered during our investigation, including new witnesses uncovered by Neville Scullion, to the NSW Police Homicide Squad. They have assured us that the case is still active and that they are pursuing new lines of inquiry.

In October 2022, the NSW Government together with the NSW Police Force announced a $500,000 reward for information into the suspicious disappearance of Lynette Melbin. Her case remains an active investigation.

7

Bodies in a Bag

Dawn Street & Linda Whitton

People disappear for a variety of reasons – whether voluntarily, to start new lives, or due to misadventure, accident or foul play. Over the years I've reported on hundreds of missing person cases, from runaway teenagers to elderly people with dementia who've become confused and lost, to other cases where something more sinister has occurred.

I have only ever had two careers in my life: cop and journalist. These are two careers where you get to see up close and personal some pretty harrowing things. I've seen the dark side of life, and after a while you tend to expect the worst, so in the end not much surprises you. But there are stories that stand out from the bunch, stories that shock even the most hardened cop or battle-weary journalist due to their sheer brutality. This next story is one of those.

It was December 1993, a week before Christmas on a bright sunny day on Sydney's affluent lower north shore. At Berry Island Reserve, a delightful harbourside park with bushland, picnic areas and a rocky foreshore, families were out enjoying the sunshine. As laughing children played, this picture-perfect location was the last place you would expect to find evil. But what was uncovered here would launch one of the most bizarre criminal cases in the history of NSW Police.

For Detective Ian Lynch of the homicide squad, the tranquility of that sunny day was shattered when he received an urgent call. A body had been discovered inside a striped laundry bag partially buried under a cluster of trees. A group of children had been playing cricket, and when one ran into bushes to retrieve the ball, he'd spotted the laundry bag. Noticing a dark liquid seeping through the material, he'd opened the bag and received the fright of his life.

Inside the bag was the body of a young woman, her tiny frame naked and folded like a pretzel. Police later reported that the victim, in her 20s, had been stuffed inside the bag, which was covered by leaves and partially buried under a boulder.

The state of decomposition was advanced, but forensic police managed to identify the woman. A single fingerprint revealed her identity: Dawn Street.

Dawn was from Victoria, and the local police there had a history with her husband, Eddie. A few years earlier, Eddie had been charged with sexually assaulting his wife. Victoria police told Ian Lynch that the couple had reconciled then left Victoria and were known to be living in Sydney.

'There was nothing very nice about Eddie Street. He had an extensive criminal history in relation particularly to violence against women,' Ian said when I interviewed him about the case.

The detective quickly tracked down an address for the couple in Annandale, in Sydney's inner west. A police background check revealed that they were well known to local police due to frequent domestic disturbances. Dawn, a tiny woman, had often been the victim of Eddie's violent outbursts, leaving her bruised and battered.

Eddie the wife beater was heavy set, which is a polite way of saying he was solid and overweight. His face was marked by years of alcoholism. Long, dirty, greasy hair framed his ruddy complexion, his red bulbous nose a testament to his hard drinking.

When questioned by the police, Eddie told them that Dawn had taken off weeks earlier after they'd had a fight, and she had never returned. He claimed he'd reported her missing at the local police station, which checked out. Despite his record of domestic abuse, Eddie seemed to care that his wife was dead. He appeared on the television news, making an appeal for information. 'Anyone who knows anything, I'd really like to know,' he pleaded.

Ian watched the appeal repeatedly and didn't buy Eddie's sincerity. He noticed that Eddie avoided eye contact and his expressions were impassive and seemed staged. The detective had interviewed hundreds of murderers during his career, and he could pick out those telling fibs. He suspected Eddie knew more than he was letting on, but with no known cause of death due to the decomposed state of Dawn's body, and no evidence linking Eddie to her disappearance, he couldn't arrest him.

'Eddie Street claimed that his wife had left him 17 days before the discovery of her body. He was able to nominate a TV show they were both watching that night. They'd both watched the show. He said he'd gone to have a shower and when he came out she was gone, and he hadn't seen or heard from her since,' Ian remembered.

Eddie told police they'd been watching the movie *Cocoon* when Dawn took off. The detective checked the TV guide and it confirmed this part of Eddie's story. However, he was not convinced about the rest of it, so he set out to debunk Eddie's account of Dawn's disappearance.

Now, before I go on, I want to explain how I know Ian Lynch. When I joined Darlinghurst Police Station as a uniformed constable, Ian was attached to Darlinghurst detectives. A couple of years later, I transferred to the detectives' office, which had moved into the newly minted Sydney Police Centre. On my first day, Ian asked me out for a chat. He proceeded to warn me about a couple of rogue detectives in the office, and told me to be careful whenever I worked with them, and to make sure I didn't get sucked into abusing and misusing the badge.

I appreciated the way Ian had looked out for me that morning, and we've remained friends since that day more than 30 years ago. He's a good guy and a brilliant investigator. He's also very imposing, standing at 1.93 metres, with broad shoulders and a sharp mind. He spent decades in the homicide squad solving some of the state's most complex and horrific murders. But he ranks the murder of Dawn Street as one of the most bizarre.

To disprove Eddie's account of Dawn's last movements, Ian began canvassing the local area, speaking to neighbours and business owners. When he visited the local chemist, he struck gold. The chemist recalled selling Eddie a camera a few weeks earlier and developing a roll of film for him that had not yet been collected. Ian asked to look at the photos. One in particular caught his eye. It showed Eddie in the flat he had shared with Dawn, with a wardrobe in the background. The wardrobe door was open, and inside was a striped laundry bag, just like the one Dawn's body had been found in.

The lead was significant but not enough to arrest Eddie. Lots of people owned the same type of laundry bag.

Then a taxi driver contacted police with crucial information. He told them that, about three weeks prior, he had picked up a man from Wollstonecraft Railway Station, near Berry Island Reserve, and that the man had been carrying a large blue suitcase. The taxi driver had driven the man to a location in Annandale, close to where Eddie and Dawn lived. During the ride, the passenger had told the driver that he'd stormed out after a fight with his wife but had decided to return home to make up.

Piece by piece, Ian Lynch built a case against Eddie Street. A local nun provided another piece of the puzzle, reporting that she'd seen Eddie and Dawn together after he'd claimed to police that she had left him and he had reported her missing. The nun remembered that Dawn had been wearing a pair of blue stretch pants. The nun's statement directly contradicted Eddie's timeline, and provided evidence of his deception, proving he'd lied to police about Dawn's disappearance.

Ian became convinced that Eddie's story of Dawn's disappearance was a smokescreen, a poorly crafted alibi to cover his tracks. Determined to find more evidence and blow Eddie's story out of the water, the detective and one of his team decided to pay Eddie a visit at his new address in a boarding house in Annandale. The police wanted to find the blue stretch pants and any other evidence that would help them build a strong circumstantial case against Eddie for Dawn's disappearance and murder.

Eddie's room was a dive, disorganised and dirty, with clothes and other items strewn around the place. During the search they found clothing belonging to Dawn.

'We searched a large bundle of clothing looking for the blue pants. It became necessary to take a lot of clothing that still belonged to Dawn back to examine elsewhere.'

The detective scanned the dimly lit room, looking for a bag to carry the clothes in. 'Two suitcases were sitting on

Edwin 'Eddie' Street (Nathan Edwards / Newspix)

the floor of the unit. We asked if we could take a suitcase to put the clothing in, and [Eddie] nominated a red suitcase which had been sitting there,' Ian told me. 'I opened the red suitcase and I said, "Well, this one's already got something in it." I opened the blue suitcase and inside that suitcase I found another suitcase. I then opened that suitcase.'

What he saw next made him recoil in horror, knocking aside the other detective. He let out a string of expletives. There, inside the suitcase, lay the lifeless, bloodstained body of a woman.

When confronted with the discovery, Eddie was nonchalant. 'That's Linda. We had a hell of a fight last night,' he explained.

Linda Whitton was Eddie's new girlfriend.

Later, in a recorded police interview, Eddie gave investigators a bizarre account of how Linda had died. 'I turned around, and she started sticking this damn knife into herself. She grabbed the knife and was plunging it in like so …' Eddie demonstrated, making thrusting motions towards his chest and stomach.

'Was the blade going into her at that particular point in time?' Ian probed.

'Well, I went to grab it,' Eddie said in a vain attempt to convince police he was innocent.

'Was she bleeding?' the detective asked.

'I didn't quite notice any blood. It happened so quick,' came Eddie's unconvincing reply.

Sure enough, the front of Linda's body had stab wounds, but Eddie could not explain the stab wound in the middle of her back. He claimed the wounds were all self-inflicted.

Then, during a second recorded interview with Ian, he confessed to killing his wife, Dawn, with a pillow.

'I took that pillow and placed it over her face,' Eddie admitted. 'I really didn't have any intention – it just seemed to happen. I just seemed to snap. I picked it up and put it over her face. All of a sudden. I didn't realise she was dead. I just put my arm around her and lay there for a while. When she didn't move, I realised something was wrong.'

Having murdered his wife, Eddie knew he had to get rid of her body and come up with a story about her disappearance. So he stuffed her into a bag and caught a cab to Wollstonecraft. At Berry Island Reserve, he found a secluded spot in the bush where he buried the striped laundry bag containing Dawn's body in a shallow grave and covered it with leaves.

The day after his arrest, police took Eddie back to the reserve, and he walked them through what he'd done.

'I dug the hole,' he began.

'You dug the hole. then what did you do?'

'I took my wife out of the suitcase and put her in the hole.'

Eddie's complete lack of compassion shocked hardened homicide detectives, including Ian. He told me it was an all too familiar story of domestic violence taken to its most horrific extreme.

In the end, Ian was able to uncover the truth, no matter how deeply Eddie had tried to bury it.

In a bizarre twist, a false lead pursued by police had become the key to cracking the case wide open. It turned out that the nun who claimed to have seen Dawn in blue stretch pants with Eddie after Dawn went missing had been mistaken. It wasn't Eddie and Dawn who she'd seen; most likely, it was Eddie and Linda.

In another strange turn, Eddie told Ian that a police car had stopped to speak to him in Wollstonecraft while he was walking to Berry Island Reserve carrying the laundry bag containing Dawn's body. The police asked what he was doing out so late and what was in the bag. Eddie explained that his missus had kicked him out, so he'd grabbed a bag full of clothes and was on his way to stay at a mate's place.

The cops never asked to look inside the bag. If they had, they would have discovered Dawn's limp body, and Eddie would have been arrested. Moreover, Linda would still have been alive.

Despite confessing to Dawn's murder, Eddie refused to admit to killing Linda, sticking to his fanciful story that she had stabbed herself to death. However, police discovered that Eddie had also filed a false missing person report about Linda and tried to mislead investigators by claiming that her violent ex-boyfriend had threatened to kill her.

At Eddie's trial, the judge and jury found his claims absurd. Based on the overwhelming evidence, Eddie was convicted of both murders and sentenced to life in prison. His papers were marked 'never to be released', ensuring he would die behind bars.

As Eddie was led from the courtroom to the cells below, he uttered the famous words of Australian bushranger Ned Kelly: 'Such is life.'

In jail, Eddie Street earned the nickname 'Suitcase'. He died from cancer in Sydney's Long Bay jail in 2007.

8

Snatched at the Footy

Joanne Ratcliffe & Kirste Gordon

Adelaide is known as the City of Churches, but concealed behind its seemingly serene facade is a dark reputation as a city of evil that has witnessed some of Australia's most horrific crimes.

It was here, among the impressive historical churches with their magnificent spires and captivating stained-glass windows, that the story of Joanne Ratcliffe and Kirste Gordon would unfold, forever changing the lives of their families and the community.

Saturday, 25 August 1973 was a crisp winter's day. Adelaide Oval was buzzing with excitement as families gathered to

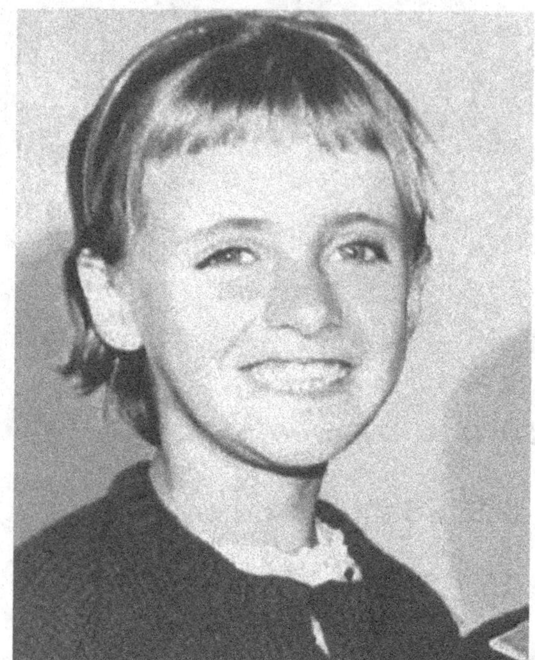

Joanne Ratcliffe

Kirste Gordon

watch a footy match between Norwood and North Adelaide. The sounds of cheering filled the air along with the familiar smells of pies and beer. Among the spectators were the Ratcliffe family, loyal Norwood supporters who religiously watched their team play every weekend. Eleven-year-old Joanne Ratcliffe, with a thick mane of auburn hair and a heart full of youthful enthusiasm, was there with her parents, Les and Kathleen, and her older brother, David.

As the game progressed, Joanne befriended four-year-old Kirste Gordon, a bright-eyed little girl whose grandmother, Rita, was sitting in the same area. Rita was babysitting Kirste while her parents were away for the weekend. Seeing that the adults were engrossed in the game, Joanne, who was quite mature for her age, took Kirste under her wing. Despite their age difference, the two girls were drawn to each other.

At one point during the game, Joanne offered to take the little girl to the toilet. The trip was uneventful, and the girls returned to their seats without incident. But around 3.45 pm the girls made a second trip to the toilet. This time they never came back.

Sensing something was wrong, the Ratcliffes began to frantically search the oval. Joanne's mum, dad and brother scoured the stands, retracing the steps they believed Joanne would have taken. Then they combed through grassy areas and the tennis courts behind the stands, which Joanne and David knew well, but there was no sign of the girls.

Desperate, Joanne's mother approached the announcers' booth, pleading for an announcement to be made over the PA system, but her request was coldly refused. The game was in full swing, and the announcer insisted it would be pointless, as no one would hear it over the roar of the crowd. He told Joanne's mother to wait until the final siren, and appeared not to take her concerns seriously. But the situation was grave. Joanne's mother knew her daughter was a very responsible child, and when given a job to do, she'd stick to it.

The minutes ticked by excruciatingly slowly. It wasn't until 5.15 pm that the announcement about the missing girls was finally made. A vital 90 minutes had been lost and by then it was too late. The crowd had begun to disperse, the oval was nearly empty, and the girls were gone.

The police were called and they descended on the oval, speaking to anyone who was still there. One witness told a television reporter she'd seen the girls walking behind a man: 'The girls were behind him, a little bit to the left. They walked up towards the southern entrance gate.' Another witness recalled seeing an older, thin man with a distinctive hat carrying a distressed Kirste while Joanne bravely followed behind, screaming at the man to put her friend down and hitting him, trying desperately to free Kirste.

Other than being thin and wearing an uncommon hat, descriptions of the man were vague. He was a ghostly figure, calm and confident. His demeanour suggested this was not the first time he had attempted such a heinous act.

The chilling reality was that this mystery man, who witnesses said had his hat pushed low to conceal his face, had likely been watching and waiting for the perfect moment to strike. He was an opportunistic predator who had seen an opportunity in Kirste, a small vulnerable child, and taken it. He struck with terrifying speed, sweeping Kirste up and carrying her away, as if she was nothing more than an object to be stolen.

It seemed that Joanne, who was playing the role of big sister that day, was collateral damage. She was only 11 years old, but she showed bravery beyond her years. When Kirste was seized, she ran after the predator, calling out for him to stop and trying everything she could to save her young friend. She was fierce and unrelenting, clinging to her friend and refusing to let the man separate them. She pulled, fought and did everything in her power to protect Kirste. She could have saved herself, but she refused to leave Kirste, and her courage sadly sealed her fate.

In that act Joanne became more than a friend, she became a protector, determined to stand between her young friend and the unthinkable. Joanne's selfless act is hard to comprehend, especially in one so young.

Despite Joanne's ruckus, no one got involved or checked to see what was going on. You see, onlookers presumed that Joanne and Kirste were little girls behaving badly, and that the man was a relative, so no one intervened to help them.

It was utterly tragic that, in a crowd of thousands, everyone turned a blind eye to two little girls in distress. Call it urban apathy but, looking back, I think it was tragic and appalling. I can imagine Joanne and Kirste screaming and fighting to break free and being ignored. How must they have felt? It breaks my heart just to think about it.

I vividly remember watching the news stories about the girls' abduction. Although I lived in another state, the story was broadcast around the country. I was about the same age as Joanne and I recall being terrified of the same thing happening to me. When you're a kid, stories like this reinforce fears of the bogeyman, the mythical creature that terrorises children.

I had many sleepless nights worried someone would come and take me.

After the 50th anniversary of the girls' disappearance came and went in 2023, I decided to look into the case and discover what leads had surfaced over all those years. The passing of time is not an excuse to forget. Sure, those responsible may no longer be alive, but Joanne and Kirste deserve justice, and their families deserve answers and the chance to bring them home and lay them to rest.

Suzie Ratcliffe was born 14 months after her sister, Joanne, disappeared. Her parents had wanted another child, to try to fill the void left when Joanne went missing. Suzie grew up in the shadow of a sister she never knew but felt deeply connected to. Her sister's absence was a constant presence in the Ratcliffe household. 'I was about three and a half when I found out,' Suzie told me when we met at her home in Mount Evelyn, a semi-rural area an hour outside of Melbourne. 'We had the mantelpiece over the fireplace, and on that we had lots of photos, and one prominent photo was of my brother and Joanne. I would always question my mum and dad about who that little girl was with my brother.'

As a young girl, Suzie would sneak out of her bedroom at night, long after everyone else had gone to bed, and sit by the mantelpiece, talking to the photo of her sister. 'I'd hear Mum and Dad crying in their bedroom and they'd try to muffle it because they didn't want to upset my brother or myself,' she told me.

Suzie said her father spent years searching for Joanne. 'He would come home, have a shower, get a bite to eat and then go driving around Adelaide, just stopping and asking people if they'd seen anything or heard anything,' Suzie recalled. 'I will never forget the haunted look on his face. Like, even on days when he tried to put on the bravest face and act happy, you could still see the sadness in his eyes.'

Her brother, David, was just 13 years old when Joanne was taken, and his younger sister's abduction weighed on him for the rest of his life. Suzie said David never forgave himself for not being there when the girls were taken. 'He blamed himself,' Suzie said quietly. 'Right up until the time he died in 2020 he carried that guilt for not going with the girls to the toilet, for not bringing them back safely.'

The loss of a child causes a wound that never heals, but when a child disappears without a trace and under frightening circumstances, the pain is even more intense. It's a constant gnawing agony, a question that is never answered. It's like treading water in a pool of uncertainty and it never gets easier.

Suzie has kept some of Joanne's toys as well as folders full of newspaper articles and other papers about the case, and when I visited her she'd laid them all out on a coffee table.

She picked up an envelope and removed a letter written by her father shortly before he died of cancer, in which he pleaded for information into Joanne and Kirste's disappearance.

Suzie unfolded the letter and, struggling to contain her emotions, read it out to me. 'The doctors have told me that I will be dead of cancer within a matter of a few weeks from now. That is unless a miracle happens. It will not happen.' Suzie paused before continuing. 'I want to know what happened that day at the Adelaide Oval. It will have been worthwhile if, before I go, I know what happened to Joanne. Even if someone could tell me where her body is, that would be enough.'

Les Ratcliffe's words were a heartbreaking testament to his determination never to stop searching, never to stop hoping, right up until his final breath. Towards the end of the letter, Les made a direct appeal to the abductor. 'Before I die, I want to know what happened to my little girl. Wherever you are, abductor, my telephone number is —' and he stated the number. 'You too will be meeting your maker.'

Les Ratcliffe's final wish wasn't granted. He died without knowing what had happened to Joanne. 'He was diagnosed with cancer in December 1980,' Suzie said, clutching the letter and staring at her father's sombre words. 'It was aggressive pancreatic cancer,' she said, her voice cracking with emotion. 'He passed away on the 2nd of February 1981.'

Suzie had spent every day since her father's death trying to fulfil his dying wish. Over the years, police had followed thousands of lines of inquiry but the case remained unsolved. But Suzie's determination had never wavered, and now she believed she knew who had taken Joanne and Kirstie, thanks to an extensive investigation by Adelaide journalist Bryan Littlely. Like Suzie, Bryan wasn't born when the girls went missing, but once he began to look into the case, he wouldn't let it go.

Bryan's research into the case centred on a notorious paedophile named Stanley Arthur Hart. Bryan discovered that Hart had had access to various properties around Adelaide, and at one time might have lived not far from Kirste's grandmother, making it possible that he had seen the little girl before that fateful day at the footy.

In 2009, while working for the *Adelaide Advertiser* newspaper, Bryan received a mysterious package. Inside was a 63-page handwritten confession from a convicted paedophile named Mark Trevor Marshall, the grandson of Stanley Arthur

Hart. The document contained disturbing details, diagrams and a map. It was a chilling account of what had happened to Joanne and Kirste.

'Joanne was still alive when they came home, after the first girl died,' Marshall wrote. 'She came out in the morning and told me that she was allowed to live, and then within half a day she was dead.'

Marshall alleged that his grandfather, Stanley, had abducted the girls and taken them to a remote farm, where they were subjected to unspeakable horrors before they were murdered. Their bodies, he claimed, were dismembered and placed in barrels full of acid, which were then hidden.

Mark Trevor Marshall's confession to a Christian prison worker while in jail for child sex offences was subsequently submitted to the Mullighan Inquiry, which looked into the widespread sexual abuse of children in state care in South Australia between 2004 and 2008.

Marshall had been called before the inquiry in March 2007, and been interviewed by Commissioner Edward Mullighan. Like his written confession, his evidence to the Mullighan Inquiry contained startling allegations about his grandfather.

Stanley Arthur Hart had a dark past. His history is riddled with violence and cruelty. In 1966 he had been convicted of abusing an 11-year-old girl, and his wife had apparently died of starvation due to being kept prisoner on their remote farm at Yatina, about 220 kilometres north of Adelaide.

In the *South Australian Government Gazette* of 28 April 1966, Hart stood accused of two counts of carnal knowledge, indecent assault, and gross indecency in the presence of a female under 16 years.

Hart was a butcher by trade, a detail that has horrific implications in light of Marshall's handwritten confession. I have a copy and it makes for sobering reading. His writing looks childlike and is at times chaotic and filled with ramblings. But among the incoherent and erratic scribbles are details that Bryan has been able to verify. Most significant is a map that Marshall drew in which he marked the spot where he claimed the barrels containing the girls' remains were hidden. He alleged the girls had been buried in a service tunnel near a reservoir close to the Hart farm.

When I first heard about this development, I decided that I needed to find out more and check the veracity of Marshall's claims. So, in early 2023, I flew to Adelaide to interview Bryan about what he had uncovered. We had arranged to meet in the foyer of the hotel I was staying at. When I went down to see him, I discovered he had another man with him who he introduced as Brad Gardam.

My first impression was that Bryan and Brad were a couple of rough nuts. Both were dressed in jeans, T-shirts and leather jackets. Inside the hotel they took off their jackets to reveal heavily tattooed arms and it would have been obvious to any onlooker that they were into motorbikes – Bryan was holding a helmet and wearing bike boots, while Brad's T-shirt said 'Jester Motorcycle Club'. I noticed Brad was carrying a blue plastic bag, but I couldn't see what was inside.

Brad began by telling me that he had a personal connection to the case, a claim that stunned me. 'How?' I asked.

He told me that he'd known Hart's family when he was a young teenager and had crossed paths with them at his parents' property. 'The last weekend of the September school holidays in 1981, Mark Marshall's brother stayed on our farm, and Hart came to our farm to pick him up.'

This revelation caught me off guard. I hadn't been expecting Bryan to bring Brad along to our meeting, and I certainly did not expect Brad to have had contact with the main suspect in the case.

Brad explained to me that he had come into possession of Marshall's confession some years earlier. It was in late 2008 –

he thought December – and he was at a friend's tattoo parlour when his mate handed him a pile of documents that had been given to him by someone with connections to the Gypsy Joker Motorcycle Club. 'Have a read of this,' his friend said. Brad took the documents home and was immediately drawn into the dark world of Marshall's confession.

Like most people born in Adelaide, Brad had heard about the girls' abduction. 'My initial reaction was, "Oh my God, I know these people!"' he told me, still full of disbelief at the connection. 'I crossed paths with them when I was in high school.'

Brad said he couldn't shake the feeling that he had to do something, so he did. 'I loaded a small truck up with slings and blocks and all sorts of equipment and a sludge pump,' he said. Brad enlisted a couple of his mates to help him, and they followed the map drawn by Marshall. It took them to a bush location about 20 kilometres from Hart's old farm.

Brad said they came to what looked like the entrance to a tunnel, but he couldn't be sure because it was covered with overgrown vegetation. So he and his mates smashed through the overgrowth, exposing a tunnel behind it. 'Very overgrown area and extremely difficult to get to,' he explained.

Once they had cleared the entrance, Brad stepped inside the tunnel. There he found two barrels. They were covered in grime and hidden away from the world, a dark secret concealed for decades. 'One of the barrels was at the entrance of the tunnel. It was partly under water and had floated to the entrance. And the other one was far back, deep into the tunnel. So we pumped [the tunnel] all day ... and it was still four feet deep.'

Brad said he pulled the barrels out and peeled back the rusted lids with frightened trepidation. I asked him to describe what was inside. 'It was like a dense honeycomb and blood-coloured substance that sparkled in the sunlight,' he said.

Brad took samples of the contents from both barrels back home, and then asked a veterinarian he knew to conduct tests to determine the presence of blood. 'He did what you call strip tests on them, and the first test came back positive for blood,' Brad said.

He didn't want to jump to conclusions, so he insisted the vet use different batches of test strips to double-check his findings. 'He did them with three different batches, and each and every one of those batches of test strips came back positive for blood.'

The vet used Multistix 9 urine strips in the analysis. The strips test for ten important markers found in the human body, including blood. While the tests were not conclusive, they did show a faint trace of blood, and a high acidity level that potentially pointed to something horrible. According to Marshall's confession, Joanne and Kirste were dismembered after they were killed and put in barrels full of acid to dissolve their bodies.

As I listened to Brad explain to me what he'd done, I wondered why he'd gone to such great lengths. 'Mate, most people wouldn't have done what you did. They would have ignored Marshall's confession,' I told him. 'Most people would have gone, "It's bullshit." Why didn't you?'

It was a question that invited suspicion, but it was relevant. I had to know what his motivation was, because it would determine the veracity of what he was telling me. It's my job to ask questions, even uncomfortable ones.

Following my question I felt a change in Brad's demeanour. He dropped his head and I sensed I had unearthed a secret he'd buried deep inside himself for many years. His voice faltered as he began to recount how a young female relative of his had been molested by someone connected to Marshall's family. 'What compelled me to sink my teeth into this was that I had been affected by these very people,' he said softly. '[Name redacted] sexually molested my nine-year-old relative, and I've kept tabs on him ever since. I still to this day know where he is.'

'So it was personal?' I asked him point-blank.

'Yeah,' he answered softly.

Brad had been 13 or 14 at the time, just a kid himself, and he'd been unable to protect her. The guilt had eaten away at him ever since, and he saw the case of Joanne and Kirste as a chance to finally make things right, to deliver justice for them, even if he hadn't been able to deliver justice for his young relative.

I could tell that the pain was still raw and keenly felt. Brad had never shared this story with anyone before, and talking about it for the first time was hard, but it had been a driving motivation to keep fighting to find out what happened to Joanne and Kirste, and it answered my question about why he'd gone to so much trouble. 'For the last 40-odd years, I partly blame myself for what happened. I could have prevented it in hindsight,' Brad lamented.

Brad had taken the samples from the barrels to the South Australia Police so they could conduct their own more extensive tests. He had handed the samples over in the presence of a lawyer, and asked to be given a receipt. But later, when he followed up on what was happening, he said he was told by an investigator that they'd 'lost the evidence'.

Brad had been flabbergasted. How could the police lose potential evidence connected to one of the highest-profile unsolved cases in Australia? He admitted that his resolve was shaken, until one day in 2011 when he saw a newspaper article that reignited the fire within him. 'I was at the halfway point in the paper, and there was a little section about this confession and the story was written by an investigative journalist called Bryan Littlely.'

Bryan's story centred on Marshall's confession. So, without a second thought, Brad called the *Adelaide Advertiser* and demanded to speak to Bryan.

The two men came together through what can only be described as fate, inexplicably connected by the same horrific crime. They had both independently come into possession of Marshall's confession. When Brad told Bryan about the existence of the barrels, Bryan was blown away. But there were more bombshell revelations to come.

After discovering the barrels, Brad had searched Hart's abandoned farm, and inside a dusty old shed he'd made a chilling discovery. He'd found two old hats, one of which matched the description given by witnesses of the hat worn by the abductor. It was a Royal Stetson, a hat not commonly worn by men in Adelaide back in 1973. One eyewitness had said at the time: 'That's one thing that won't go out of my mind is the hat. The hat sat on his head straight, the brim was straight out, and it sat like this on the top of his head.'

From the beginning, the hat had been an identifying feature of the girls' abductor.

The second hat Brad found was an army slouch hat. Both hats were weathered, worn and had been discarded by their former owner before being found again. Each stitch and fray held a dark secret.

Brad had brought the slouch hat with him to our meeting. It was inside the blue plastic bag he was carrying. The hat looked like a relic from the past, like something you would find in a museum. But both men were convinced that the combination of the slouch hat and the Royal Stetson amounted to a compelling circumstantial case against Stanley Arthur Hart.

I asked Brad why the slouch hat was significant, when witnesses claimed the abductor had been wearing a Royal Stetson hat.

Brad held the slouch hat up in front of me. 'It's an old army slouch hat, and the leather banding has been removed from the inside and outside.' He ran his finger along the rim where the leather had once been. 'The Royal Stetson hat, which resembled the one worn by the person who took the children, has strips of leather on it.'

'So we've got two hats,' I said. 'The one worn by the abductor and this old army hat that you're holding. And you believe the leather stripping was taken from one and put on the other, is that right?'

'That's a fair statement,' Brad said. 'That is what appears to have occurred.'

Brad said that he had been able to confirm that Stanley Arthur Hart was a veteran who served in World War II: his headstone bears the inscription 'a grateful country thanks you' with the rising sun on it.

Bryan Littlely gave the Stetson hat to South Australian police on 19 August 2023. He received a police property receipt, which he showed me. However, despite Bryan and Brad's relentless efforts and Suzie Ratcliffe's steely determination and resolve, the South Australia Police seem uninterested in the new evidence, in particular the barrels. They have never asked to take a sample from the barrels to conduct their own forensic tests so they could determine once and for all whether the contents do in fact contain human blood. DNA technology has advanced significantly over recent times, so there is a very good chance that they could extract a profile.

Bryan believes Marshall is telling the truth, because you can't make this stuff up. 'There's no way those barrels could have got there in any other way. One hell of a bloody prank to pull if you can do that. So that's rock-solid,' Bryan insisted.

Officially, the police have dismissed Marshall's confession as 'fantasy', which I find odd because in 2012 they conducted extensive searches of two Yatina properties, including Stan Hart's old farm, not once, not twice, but three times.

In a press conference at that time, then Detective Inspector Greg Hutchins said this about the raids police carried out: 'South Australia Police have continued their investigation into the 1973 kidnapping of Joanne Ratcliffe, aged 11, and Kirste Gordon, aged four years old, from the Adelaide Oval. This week we attended several sites at a property at Yatina, where we spent three days excavating a well and examining a second well. This is after a number of visits to the location over the past 12 months.'

Suzie Ratcliffe has accused South Australia Police of stonewalling, and she's been frustrated and disappointed by their lack of transparency. Bryan, too, cannot understand why they have not pursued the barrel lead. Of course, police may have very good reasons for wanting to keep parts of an investigation confidential, but Bryan and Brad could have crucial evidence that solves the case. They have both said that they are willing to be proven wrong, but police have thus far refused to do that.

'We've got a confession. We've got what I think is hard and fast evidence that could be tested to be eliminated. We've got modus operandi – he's done this before,' Bryan said, frustrated.

And we have police searching Hart's farm, and police have taken possession of a hat found in a shed on Hart's abandoned farm.

I have been out of the police force for a long time, and I'm sure that things have changed a lot, but I cannot help feeling that there is a reluctance by police to follow up good leads. I contacted South Australia Police to get their side of the story. I was prepared for them to tell me that Bryan and Brad are off the mark, but they refused to make any comment. In an email I received from South Australia Police they wrote: 'We recognise the value of utilising the media in unsolved homicides and have a media strategy for our unsolved cases, however, we will not be participating at this time.'

A media strategy for our unsolved cases. Well, whatever that strategy is, it's not working, because 50 years have passed and the police are still no closer to solving this case.

Bryan believes the police are hiding something, and he's convinced that the man who took Kirste and Joanne is

Stanley Arthur Hart. 'Well, the evidence tells me that Hart was responsible. I think that's logical. There are too many ticks in too many boxes that single out Hart.'

It's been more than ten years since Brad discovered the barrels. Today, they are stored in a safe place outside Adelaide awaiting further tests. Bryan says he will happily hand them over to police. 'It's always been open to the police to take them. They have been offered to them time and time again. So why haven't they done it yet?'

* * *

Yet another key piece of evidence revealed to me by Bryan was the account of eyewitness Anthony Kilmartin. Back on that fateful day in 1973, Kilmartin was a 13-year-old kid who was selling lollies outside Adelaide Oval during the footy game. The abduction of Joanne and Kirste occurred just metres from where Kilmartin was standing, and he got the best view of the abductor. He saw the violent way the man grabbed the younger girl, and the older girl's desperate attempts to free her friend. Kilmartin spoke to police and provided a description of the abductor, which police used to produce a sketch of the man that was then circulated to the public.

Bryan told me he knew of Kilmartin as a witness but had never spoken to him until 2021, when Kilmartin contacted him after he saw Bryan on the news discussing the case. The two men met up at an Adelaide cafe and Bryan told me he could tell that Kilmartin remained haunted by the events of 50 years ago.

During the meeting, Bryan showed Kilmartin the Royal Stetson that Brad had found at Hart's farm. '[He] went white. He got emotional and he said, "That's the hat that the abductor was wearing." He also said that Stan Hart is the most likely person that he has seen fitting the police description.'

After meeting with Bryan and Brad, I too became convinced that Stanley Arthur Hart was the most likely suspect. However, I wanted another opinion. I wanted to speak to someone who could convince me that Hart wasn't responsible. If there were flaws in Bryan and Brad's investigation and I had missed them, I wanted someone to point them out.

So, before leaving Adelaide, I arranged to meet South Australian cop turned private investigator Bill Hayes. Bill was a highly regarded investigator who spent years in the police force reviewing cold cases, including the infamous disappearance of the Beaumont children from Glenelg Beach in 1966. He had no ties to the Adelaide Oval abduction case, but he had scrutinised the case, particularly Bryan and Brad's contribution, running fresh eyes over the evidence they had uncovered.

Bill lived a couple of hours outside of Adelaide on the coast. As I drove to his house I felt nervous because I knew that whatever he had to say could potentially pour cold water over everything Bryan and Brad had told me.

The drive took me on long winding roads that curved past lush vineyards, the scenery a stark contrast to the dark secrets I had come to Adelaide to uncover. I pulled up at a two-storey house nestled behind sand dunes. Waves crashed nearby.

Bill was waiting out the front. He was a tall man with what I would describe as wise eyes. After we shook hands he led me inside his house and upstairs to a room that showcased water views beyond the sand hills.

Bill gestured for me to sit down at a dining table and after we both got comfortable I cut to the chase. 'Bill, do you think Stanley Arthur Hart is responsible for the girls going missing?'

Bill didn't hesitate. 'Without a doubt it's Hart. Without a doubt.'

I pressed him on why he seemed so confident that Hart was the one.

'One really big part for me was the hat,' Bill began. 'The hat was described by a groundsman, who saw someone wearing it loitering near the ladies' toilets. Then you have young Anthony Kilmartin, who saw the abduction occurring. He saw the abductor and the hat, and I know it's been shown to him and he's had a very emotional response to seeing the hat. It is a very unique-looking hat, and that really points the finger at Hart.'

Bill was convinced that Bryan, Brad and Suzie are all on the right track, and he said that he hoped the case was close to a resolution for the sake of both girls' families. 'With Jo and Kirste, it would be good to give them a decent burial, they deserve that, not to be chucked in a hole or a barrel somewhere forgotten.'

Before I left Bill, I asked him about Adelaide's sordid reputation, a reputation that had been cemented by decades of unsolved cases involving children, and whispered rumours of paedophile rings operating with impunity.

Bill raised his gaze from the table and looked directly at me. He stretched his back to sit up straight, then delivered some blistering home truths about the City of Churches. 'There's an open seeping wound in South Australia with the loss of all these little children that have been taken. That wound needs to be cleaned and closed,' he said, his voice rising. 'Paedophile groups abusing children in South Australia are massive. I compare the Adelaide abuse scene to a duck on water. Adelaide on the surface is calm and serene, but beneath the surface, the duck's paddling like crazy. It's a massive problem and we have hundreds of them in this state for some reason. We are the state of bizarre murders and abuse of children, and they need to be properly investigated.'

I asked Bill if he believed that the sordid, depraved abuse of children still went on.

'Nothing has changed,' Bill said, his voice heavy with resignation. 'These networks still exist at all levels of society, and the higher up they are, the less chance there is of getting them.'

Bill's words made me think of the notorious Family Murders in the 1970s and 1980s, in which a group of paedophiles kidnapped, tortured, sexually abused and murdered five young boys and men. Only one man, Bevan Spencer von Einem, was ever convicted of the crimes, but police always suspected many more were involved, including some high-profile, well-known people.

I left Adelaide with a heavy heart. I had learned more than I'd ever wanted to about the city's dark side, but I was now part of the quest to find the truth. The families of Joanne and Kirste needed answers and I was determined to help find them.

* * *

Suzie Ratcliffe has spent most of her life trying to solve the disappearance of the sister she never met. Her parents and brother have all died, and although she has a daughter now, she knows the search for answers will most probably end when she dies.

In recent years, she's been battling cancer, but she has refused to let it slow her down. Together with Bryan Littlely, she has started a support group for families of missing people called 'Leave a Light On', to help other families cope with the loss of a missing loved one.

Kirste Gordon's parents, Christine and Greg, are still alive, and I am sure they too would like to bring their daughter home and lay her to rest.

Stanley Arthur Hart died in 1999, and given how many years have passed, it is quite possible that anyone else involved in the abductions of Joanne and Kirste is also dead. However, I believe that whoever was responsible may have told someone over the years what they did. That would be a heavy burden to carry – something so terrible held for so long. I cannot imagine grappling with such a dark secret.

It is never too late for someone to unburden themselves of the guilt they have carried. I hope that someone who knows something reads this and decides to do the right thing.

There is a $1 million reward on offer for information about the case, which is a life-changing amount of money, if that is someone's motivation.

In March 2025, a private search commenced in the area around the tunnels where the barrels were located. South Australia Police told the media they had previously searched in that location and did not believe there was enough evidence to warrant further exploration.

Meanwhile, Suzie Ratcliffe has vowed to never give up. She has this message for anyone who may know something.

'We've been robbed of two beautiful girls who had their whole lives ahead of them. Both families were denied the opportunity to watch their daughters grow up, to go to high school, to fall in love, get married, have children of their own and do whatever they wanted in life. And it just strengthens my resolve that we're going to end this.'

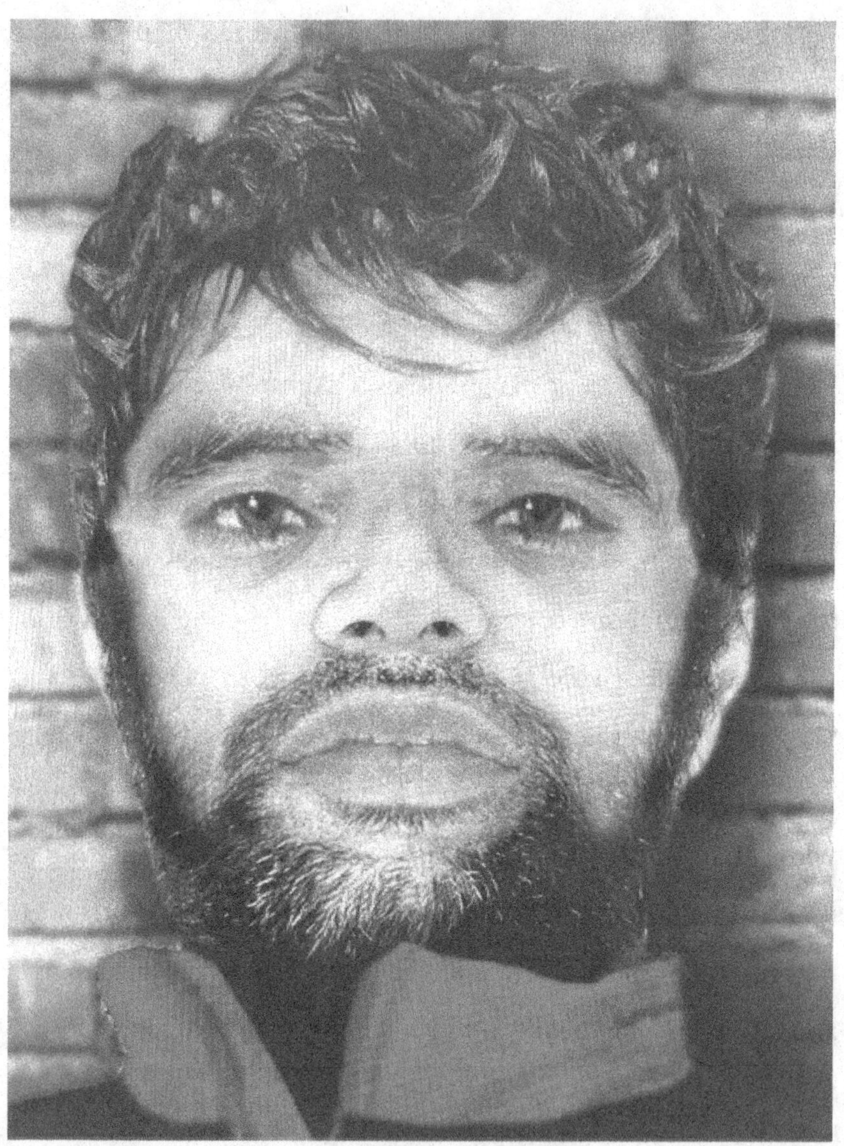

A mock-up of the Pakenham Man (Victoria Police)

9

Ghost on the Platform

The Pakenham Man

Detective Sergeant Mick Van Der Heyden of the Victoria Police felt a deep sadness as he stared at the missing person file he had been given. The cold hard facts of the case were disturbing. A man had died alone in 2008 and here he was, more than a decade later, still without a name. His life had ended on the tracks of Pakenham Railway Station on the outskirts of Melbourne, yet no family had come forward to claim him or mourn him. It was as though he never meant anything to anyone.

The media dubbed him 'the Pakenham Man' and the case had become one of Victoria's most baffling missing person mysteries.

Police know how and when he died, but not why. They also don't know who he is, and no one has come forward to say they recognise him. Imagine dying, with no one seeming to care.

I first learned of the case in 2023. The Pakenham Man and his unfinished story worried me, so I had to try to find out who this man was. I had to try to give him a name so that he had some basic dignity in death. I had to make sure he was not forgotten.

I contacted Detective Sergeant Mick Van Der Heyden and travelled to Melbourne to meet him and learn whatever I could about the case. We met in the carpark of Pakenham Police Station.

Mick had driven 100 kilometres just to speak to me. His voice was steady as he recounted the details of the case, but I could see the burden of it in his eyes. 'I actually felt a lot of sadness,' Mick admitted of how he felt when he started working on the investigation in 2016. 'This poor guy had, you know, unfortunately passed away in 2008 and, years on, we're still without a name that we could give him and provide answers to a family. So I was actually quite saddened, but it really piqued my interest because I enjoy the protracted investigations for missing persons or unidentified remains.'

This was not just another case for him; it had become a mission. He had taken over the investigation nearly eight years after the man's death and had made a fresh public appeal. Yet, despite his efforts, no one had come forward with new information.

The more I listened, the more it reinforced how little was known about the Pakenham Man. But, ironically, the last minutes of his life had been recorded in living colour, frame by frame on CCTV.

The evening of Thursday, 14 August 2008 was cold, and Pakenham Railway Station was nearly deserted. At 8.50 pm, CCTV cameras captured the unknown man for the first time. The grainy footage showed him walking onto the platform, his figure slightly hunched as if he were carrying the weight of the world. He was unshaven, with dark hair, dressed in baggy blue jeans and a red sports jacket. Although his face was partially obscured by glasses, his brown skin suggested he was of Pakistani or Indian descent.

For a few moments the man simply stood there, a lone figure in the emptiness of the train station. His only company, an empty train standing alongside one of the platforms, waiting to disembark. Then the man entered the third carriage of the stationary train and was filmed on the train's CCTV.

Mick described the footage in chilling detail. 'He stays in the carriage for about seven minutes. During that time, he stands up, he holds the railing, he sits down, obviously maybe conflicted in his mind about what his intentions are, what he's planning on doing. After that seven-minute period, he goes back onto the platform and the footage cuts out, so he disappears.'

Mick paused, his voice heavy with the burden of what came next. 'He reappears at about 9.09 pm, so we're talking 20 minutes since he's arrived, and you see him standing between the coupling of the third and fourth carriages where, again, the footage cuts out and he disappears from view. The theory, consistent with the evidence, is that he climbed down onto the platform and laid himself between the third and fourth carriage. That train departed, I believe, at about 9.18 pm, so we're talking 28 minutes to half an hour after he arrived. And that train departed, to head towards Melbourne, and unfortunately ended his life.'

The footage was as distressing as Mick described. It was dark and the man was by himself. I viewed the haunting footage over and over again, trying to make sense of what this obviously tormented man must have been feeling. There is no sound to accompany the vision, just colour pictures that tell a story of a man all alone. A man who walks aimlessly along the platform before stepping inside an empty carriage then out again, while preparing to take his own life.

'I can almost feel how he was feeling,' Mick continued, his voice filled with sadness. 'I can just sort of see the pain that he had about the decision he was about to make. So it can be distressing to watch, knowing what the outcome is. But it's the sort of thing, you know, in hindsight, I wish someone could have been there for him to help him get out of the situation and give him the help that he actually needed at that time.'

Despite Mick's efforts, identifying the man proved to be a huge challenge. The man had no ID on him, no tattoos, no scars that police could follow up on. They started to think he might have come from overseas, possibly arriving in Australia as a refugee, or maybe he had overstayed his visa and was in the country illegally. But all these theories came up empty.

I asked Mick if he thought that Pakenham locals might have known the man but were reluctant to come forward, fearing trouble if they were visa overstayers or had employed him illegally.

Mick nodded thoughtfully. 'Interesting question,' he replied. 'I had this discussion with the original investigator, Phil Jury. Of course, they may not want to assist the police [because they're] worried about themselves. Phil made quite a lot of inquiries with the local communities about that very issue, and gave them a bit of leeway – "We're not here to investigate visa breaches or overstaying issues. We're here to identify this person." So Phil is very confident that the community around here at the time didn't know him, based on the pretty confronting conversations he had to have with them about trying to identify a dead person, and telling them that it's not something that we're going to pursue for visa issues or anything like that. I'm pretty confident that it was dealt with accordingly at the time.'

Pakenham had, and still has, a large Indian population working in farming and hospitality. Mick and his team checked all the usual places, showing the man's photo, but no one recognised him. They even found a bank card embedded in the man's clothing, sparking hope they would find out who he was, but it belonged to another man, who worked at a local restaurant and was found alive and well. It appeared this man had lost his card, most likely on or near the tracks, and it had become entangled in the clothing of the unnamed man.

It seemed impossible that no one knew this man. It was as if he had been a ghost, passing through Pakenham unnoticed and unremembered. Mick expressed disbelief that in such a tight-knit community, the man could remain anonymous. 'No one seems to know this guy, which is very sad, and it's quite unbelievable.'

At the time of his death, the man was wearing a distinctive sports jacket with a football club logo reading 'Valley Statesman RLFC' (a rugby league football club in the ACT). Mick said it was a strong lead early in the investigation and police were hopeful it would crack the case wide open.

'We actually managed to track down the coach of the Valley Statesman, and he gave us the name of a person who had moved from the ACT to Victoria, a former player. We tracked that person down and he told us he'd worked in Pakenham between the end of 2007 and beginning of 2008,' Mick explained to me. 'The man told us he had a recollection of throwing the jacket in the bin, so the likely theory is that the Pakenham Man was in Pakenham in the months leading up to his death. But unfortunately, no one recognised the jacket in the local community.' This made me think that the man was possibly homeless and had rummaged through the bin looking for clothing.

The more I delved into the case, the more I felt the mystery man had a connection to the town of Pakenham. Mick said police had spent hundreds of hours studying CCTV footage, looking at every passenger who got on and off at Pakenham Station in the days leading up to the man's death. But the man never appeared in any other footage.

'He's obviously been in Pakenham somehow for some time before he actually walked or got a lift or a taxi or whatever to the train station,' Mick surmised. 'The most likely theory is he walked there from somewhere local within the Pakenham township.'

I left Pakenham Police Station that day determined to find out who the man was. But I knew it would be an uphill battle.

That thought haunted me as I drove to the Victorian Institute of Forensic Medicine, where unexpected and suspicious deaths are examined for the coroner. Here, the dead lie in rows, their lives reduced to mere remnants of flesh and bone. I was hoping to learn more about how they try to identify the unknown who come to them and learn their untold stories.

Dr Jodie Leditschke, manager of the Institute, was going to allow me a rare glimpse into her world. 'Just along the corridor is where we store all our deceased persons,' Jodie said, her voice echoing as we walked down a sterile white hallway. 'I won't actually be going into any of the areas. I'm just going to show you the general area. Before we go in there, confidentiality is the key. If you see any deceased persons whatsoever, you're not to mention it or anything else to anyone. We're going through a room: keep your head down at the first bit, then I'll tell you when you can look up.'

The smell hit me as we walked, a pungent and irritating odour that even the strongest chemicals had failed to disguise. It was overpowering, the kind of scent that lingers long after you have left. It reminded me of when I was a cop and attended a deceased person. The smell of death would infiltrate my police uniform and I would have to wash it again and again to get rid of it.

I tried to ignore the odour as I followed Jodie, focusing instead on the cold white walls, the colourless glass of the rooms we passed and the cold stainless-steel equipment set up inside.

Jodie began to explain the methodical process of handling the dead. 'We have a large room up ahead for autopsies,' she said, 'as well as other smaller suites for our specialised cases. This is where DNA is extracted if someone comes in without identification. Sometimes, even on admission, we don't have an ID, so we take a sample.'

As I mentioned, the process is disciplined and almost ritualistic. They extract a sample of blood if they can. If not, a toenail will do. If that too is impossible, then a fragment of bone will suffice. The DNA is carefully preserved because it is a fragile key to a lock that is yet to be opened. The samples are sent to the molecular biology lab, where scientists work their magic, extracting a profile from the tiny strands of genetic code.

The DNA profile of the Pakenham Man was pristine, an excellent specimen, Jodie said. It was established that the man was of Indian descent, aged between 22 and 40 years of age, about 173 centimetres tall and weighing around 63 kilograms. He was a man in the prime of his life.

The man's profile had been fed into the Victoria Police database, then the national one, but there was no match. Furthermore, no missing person report matched his description.

Having failed to find out who the man was after searching Australia, Mick Van Der Heyden searched overseas. He sent the distinct DNA profile, along with photos of the man taken from the CCTV footage and a summary of the circumstances leading up to his death, to 193 countries around the world in the hope that someone, somewhere, might recognise the Pakenham Man.

It was called a 'Black Notice', an international alert to try and identify a deceased person. It was a waiting game.

Unfortunately, there was no hit. Fingerprint and dental record checks also found no match.

I generally try to not let the cases I investigate get to me, but I must admit that sometimes it's hard. I couldn't help but think of the Pakenham Man lying on a steel gurney inside a refrigerator for years. It caused me to think of others like him who find themselves in dark places, alone and isolated in a foreign country with no one to turn to.

I decided to meet someone who might have more of an idea of what the Pakenham Man had been going through.

Suri Soni was then President of the Federation of Indian Associations of Victoria. Suri and I sat in his dining room, a warm and welcoming place that felt worlds away from the cold corridors of the mortuary I had just left. He poured me a cup of coffee, its aroma filling the room. 'The common problem across all people is the language and the cultural shock they see once they come here,' Suri told me with the knowledge of years spent helping newcomers adjust to life in Australia. 'Even though we read and hear about these things, coming face to face with reality is a big cultural shock for many people.'

As he continued, his tone became more sombre. 'The story of the Pakenham Man is all too familiar. During the Covid pandemic, I got a list of 100 students from one of the universities who were isolated with no one to talk to. Many didn't need food or material help; they just needed someone to talk to.'

Suri was shocked that the man was still unidentified. 'This is a bigger humanitarian issue,' he said, and I agreed. There is something deeply unsettling about the fact that in Australia the human remains of more than 700 lives are unidentified and unclaimed; it is a silent disaster.

Suri promised me that he would have the man's photo and description published in an online magazine for the Victorian Indian community and that he would spread the word through his social media contacts.

I left Suri with images from the CCTV footage swirling in my head. The man alone on the platform, then inside the carriage; the minutes of his life ticking away.

I wanted to retrace the Pakenham Man's last steps so I contacted Detective Mick Van Der Heyden again and asked to meet him at Pakenham Railway Station.

As Mick and I stood on the platform, he told me it was as though time had frozen. 'So, this is platform two on this side that we're at, which is where our man was last seen. You can actually see part of this carpark in the CCTV footage when he's walking around. The platform hasn't actually changed.'

A frame from the CCTV footage of the Pakenham Man (Victoria Police)

We walked past the camera that had captured the final minutes of the man's life, and I couldn't help but look up at it and stare. I began to imagine what he'd been thinking as he walked along the platform all alone. Was he scared? Was he resigned to what was going to happen? I remembered that he looked defeated, entering the empty carriage and placing his face in his hands. I wondered if he knew it was all being videoed.

I pictured him stepping down onto the tracks between the two carriages, and just waiting alone in the dark for the train to move. I stared at the tracks below, and wondered why he did it. The sound of an approaching train snapped me out of my thoughts. It was business as usual, the commuters around us oblivious to the tragedy the station had witnessed back in 2008.

I said goodbye to Mick and left Pakenham to head back to the city, but there was one more stop I wanted to make. I had found out that the man had been buried in Springvale Botanical Cemetery, Melbourne's largest, on 4 April 2012, after lying in the city mortuary for four years. I drove to the cemetery, not sure why I was going but feeling that I had to.

The cemetery spans 422 acres, a vast expanse of manicured lawns and towering trees. Gentle rain began to fall as I drove through the front gate, and the sky turned a steel-grey colour. I passed a chapel, then drove past rows and rows of headstones, some adorned with fresh flowers, others dusty and long forgotten. I followed the road to the area where all the unidentified bodies are buried.

The Packenham Man was buried next to the children's section, where a playground had been built. The sight of this made me sad. I parked the car and walked along the road and up onto the lawn. The grass was wet and soft and my shoes sank into the ground with each step. I walked cautiously, careful to ensure I didn't step on anyone's grave. Finally, I came to a place dedicated to the unknown. There were no markers or headstones to say who lay beneath. The John, Jane and Baby Does buried there were all just numbers on the cemetery database.

This is the loneliest place I've ever been to, I thought. I paused and looked around, overwhelmed by the sadness of it all. 'He's in here somewhere,' I whispered, 'and we need someone to come forward and identify him so he can go home, wherever home is.'

As I stood there in the rain, I came to realise that I was probably the first person to visit his grave. Like the other unknowns buried with him, his life had ended without recognition and without closure. This dreadful reality caused me to cry.

Identification represents one of the most basic of all human rights. As I turned to leave, I made the Pakenham Man a silent promise that I would not let his story end here. I would keep searching to give him a name, and the recognition he seemed to have been denied in life.

This was a personal tragedy not only for him but also for his family, who may still not know they have lost him.

***

The Pakenham Man died on 14 August 2008. He is described as being of Indian appearance, and was aged between 22 and 40 years. He was 173 centimetres tall and weighed about 63 kilograms. He was wearing glasses, a grey Nike T-shirt with white trim, blue jeans, white runners and a red sports jacket.

10

Missing in the Tablelands

Katie O'Shea

'You'll say, "Yeah, my mum's deceased," and they'll go, "Oh, was it cancer? Was it sudden?" Then some people will push, and you go, "No, she was murdered or she's missing."'

Lily Parmenter often finds herself having to explain her mother's absence. She's forced to pause to gather her strength before the inevitable questions that reopen a wound that has never fully healed.

'No, I don't think she's alive,' Lily told me, 'and I honestly believe it's because of someone else that she's not here today.'

Katie O'Shea

It's been almost two decades since Katie O'Shea, a loving mother of five, disappeared from Far North Queensland on 29 December 2005. A decade later, a coroner declared it likely that someone had killed her, yet the case remains unsolved.

Lily has been tirelessly searching for her mother ever since. She's spent more than half her life searching for answers, hoping against hope that she might find her mother or at least discover what happened to her.

Desperate for help, Lily first contacted me back in September 2019. I promised to look into the case, but then COVID-19 hit and everything came to a halt. Still, I was determined to make good on my promise so, in 2023, I flew down to Melbourne, where Lily lives, to finally meet her in person.

After landing at Melbourne airport, I picked up a hire car and set out on the drive to Clayton, an outer suburb about an hour away. It had taken years of phone calls and emails to get to this point. As I drove, the weight of the case settled heavily on me. It was a story full of dark corners and unanswered questions.

Katie's disappearance was not reported for almost two weeks, a delay that severely stifled the police investigation. In my experience, the first 24 hours are crucial in terms of gathering evidence and finding witnesses.

At the time Katie vanished she had left her mobile phone at her son's house and had withdrawn a few hundred dollars from an ATM. After that, there was no trace of her.

I arrived at Lily's flat, a neat and tidy place on a quiet street where she lived with her boyfriend, Steve, and their cats, Nahla and Zazu. It was good to meet Lily in person; I had seen her on television and in newspapers and magazines discussing her mum's case. She was warm and welcoming as she ushered me inside to the dining room and offered me a chair.

In the adjacent kitchen I noticed a stubby of beer with a small glass on the window ledge. 'What's with the beer stubby and glass?' I asked.

'Not for drinking,' she replied. 'It's for Mum, because that was her favourite, Coopers stout. That was the only thing she ever drank. So I've bought one. It's maybe six years old now. On her birthday I put a candle on it. That's her little birthday stout cake. I always have it out, in case she's hanging around and sees it.'

I'm not surprised by this. Over the years I've met many families of missing people who hold tightly to physical mementos of their loved ones. It's a way of staying connected, a fragile thread to the past. It's as if they fear their memories of the person might fade.

Lily's devotion to her mother was touching, and her voice broke as she spoke of how she longed to turn back time and hear her mother's voice again.

'Yeah, I'd give anything to hear her say, "Turn the music up! Yeah, baby, I love that song!" Sometimes after a while you sort of forget your loved one's voice as well. I know what it sounds like but I don't have that exact memory recall of it. So that's the other weird thing about having missing family members.' Lily paused and gently bit her lip. This wasn't easy for her. 'Because there's nothing after a certain point. You don't have anything, there are no goodbye ceremonies. Sometimes I even think, *Did I make her up, am I crazy?*'

We moved to a lounge by a coffee table and Lily showed me some family photos, precious snapshots of happier times. 'That's probably one of my favourite shots of Mum, with my little brother,' Lily said, pointing to a photo, her eyes glistening with tears. 'Yeah, I just think she looks happy in that photo.'

Lily has bought her mother a Christmas card every year, and also written letters to her mum about her achievements, special memories and dreams. 'Not a day passes without wishing you were here with us,' she wrote in one. 'My most cherished memories are of the birthday parties you put on for me. They were epic and so fondly remembered.'

Katie O'Shea did not have an easy life. She had her first baby at 16, followed by four more children with her husband before they separated. She was a free spirit, dancing to a different drum, and loving her children with all her heart. Despite their modest means, she made birthdays and Christmases special for her kids, spoiling them with little treats and lavish parties.

'She'd invite every kid in school. She'd get all these, you know, toys and Pin the Tail on the Donkey … And then she'd spend hours making food to the point where there were like three trestle tables filled with Coco Pops, honey joys and everything.'

Earlier in 2005, Katie had travelled from her home in Melbourne to Ravenshoe in Far North Queensland to visit her eldest son, Alan, and his partner, Bryer. Katie had lived in Queensland before, and this trip was a chance for her to reconnect with old friends. During the visit, she learned she was going to be a grandmother, and she planned to return to Queensland for Christmas and the birth of her grandchild.

'I still remember Mum coming home from the trip, and she's like, "Hey, can you keep a secret? And I said, "Yeah," and she's like, "I can't. You know, someone is pregnant." I think the baby was due on New Year's Day.'

Katie O'Shea with Tim, Frank, Brigid and Lily

On 17 December 2005, Katie and her 11-year-old daughter, Brigid, returned to Far North Queensland. They stayed in a tent on her best friend Loma's property, where Alan also lived. A couple of hours south-west of Cairns, the area was lush with rainforest and wetlands.

Three days after Christmas, Lily spoke to her mother over the phone. When she tried calling again on New Year's Eve, the phone went straight to voicemail. Despite knowing that there was poor reception in the area, Lily began to feel uneasy, and a knot of worry tightened in her stomach. 'I remember trying to call, just to wish her a happy New Year, but there was no answer,' Lily recalled. 'I had a sinking feeling that something wasn't right.'

On 9 January 2006, Lily received a message that her brother's baby had been born. She called Alan, asking if their mother had been in the birthing room. 'She's not here,' he replied. Alan told Lily their mother had left to visit friends on 29 December and hadn't returned.

Lily couldn't believe her mum had missed the birth of her grandchild. After all, that was the reason she'd gone to Queensland. Fear gripped Lily as she began calling around, trying to trace her mother's last known movements from 2500 kilometres away in Melbourne.

'I rang a bottle shop, I rang the pub, I rang the jail, I rang the bloody Catholic church to see if my mum would randomly go to confession. I rang bus stops, I rang literally everywhere,' Lily recalled.

But no one had seen her mother.

Finally, on 13 January 2006, two weeks after Katie had disappeared, Alan went to the police. Listening to Lily speak about it, I could hear the panic in her voice, frozen in time, so many unanswered questions still haunting her every word.

'There was always this niggling sort of thing – why didn't he report her missing sooner?' she wondered aloud. 'Why the hell didn't [he] report her missing sooner?' Lily repeated, emphasising the point.

There's no doubt that Alan's delay in reporting that his mother was missing hindered the police investigation. As I said, the first 24 hours are crucial. Lily did her best, but she was limited by being so far away.

Five days after Alan filed a missing person report, he sat down with police to be interviewed. This was the only time he would formally speak to them. He has declined all subsequent requests, and I am the only journalist to ever be given access to Alan's interview.

'Time is 10.46 am on Wednesday, January 18th, 2006,' the interviewing officer said. 'Alan, is it?'

'Yeah.'

'You look a bit different.'

'I look a bit different.'

'Yeah, mate. All this information about your mum, obviously you've been speaking to the police here ...'

'Just let me little sister know what's going on.'

'Oh, okay, how old's your little sister?'

'Ah, 19 or 20.'

'All right, and where is she?'

'Melbourne.'

'What's her name?'

'Lily O'Shea.'

'And what name do you go by?'

'Alan O'Shea.'

'Ah, Alan O'Shea. Do you use any other names?'

'Corky. That's my middle name. People started calling me that when I was younger, and now I get called that.'

The police tried to lead the conversation, but Alan seemed detached, as if he were just going through the motions and wanted it to be over as soon as possible.

'You obviously don't have any information, because you're asking me for information,' he said.

'Well, it's not that we don't have information,' the detective replied. 'The information we do have is second-hand through other police, so we'd rather speak to you face to face.'

Alan came across as frustrated and weary of recounting anything about his mother. 'Seriously, just ask me my mum's whole life story,' he said. I imagined it must have been incredibly frustrating for the police.

'Start from the beginning,' the interviewing officer said. 'Mum's from Melbourne?'

'Yeah.'

'And your mum's—'

Alan interrupted the cop. 'You're going to go through all this again.'

'Yeah, I know, mate.'

'Oh, man, I wrote it all down on paper and I just told him my life story. Seriously, just ask me my mum's whole life story.'

'And to be honest with you, you'll probably have to do it again with other police. I know it's a pain in the arse, but to try to be better, we'll just take notes. Born in Melbourne?'

'Yeah, yeah.'

'Kathleen.'

'Yeah, yeah.'

'What's her middle name?'

'Mary.'

'O'Shea.'

'Yeah.'

The cops weren't getting far, but they persisted because it was important to learn all they could about Katie and her life.

'Do you know who your mum's friends in Cairns are?' the detective asked.

'Ah, not really. I only know one or two, but they probably won't appreciate me telling you guys about it.' Alan seemed reluctant to give details, wary of involving his mother's friends.

'Okay, can I ask whether they wouldn't appreciate us going to seek information, like, to see if your mum's there?'

'Come on, man, it's like raids,' Alan said.

'Well, obviously, it's got something to do with drugs.'

'Hey.'

'It's got something to do with drugs.'

'No, it doesn't have something to do with drugs.'

'Okay, well you've lost me, 'cause the main thing that we're concerned with at the moment, Alan, is your mum's welfare,' the detective said.

Of course, whether Alan answered the cop's questions or not was entirely up to him. But it did seem odd that a son would appear not to do all he could to help find his missing mother. And I wasn't the only one who thought that. Lily, too, was stumped by her brother's attitude.

After leaving Lily's house I caught a plane to Cairns in Far North Queensland to speak to another of Katie's children, Brigid, who had accompanied her mother on the Christmas trip north. Brigid had also been one of the last people to see her mother alive. She had only been 11 years old at the time, but I was hoping she'd be able to remember key details about the days leading up to her mother's disappearance.

When I stepped off the plane in Cairns, the humid air was like a thick blanket, in stark contrast to the cool Melbourne weather I'd left behind. I navigated my way through the familiar bustle of the airport, claimed my rental car then drove west. The landscape unfolded into a tapestry of rugged mountains and sprawling rainforests, a tableau of green and brown. I navigated the winding Kuranda Range Road that cuts through the mountains.

I was unsure how the interview with Brigid would go. She had been very young when her mother went missing and this would be the first time she'd ever spoken about it publicly.

Lily, on the other hand, had frequently engaged with the media to ensure her mother's case wasn't forgotten.

I continued to Ravenshoe, a small town with a population of around 1300 people. Historically, Ravenshoe was a timber town, but in 1987 almost a million hectares of forest in the area were World Heritage listed. Today the main industries are tourism and beef and dairy farming.

I pulled up at the front of Brigid's house, which was nestled among ancient trees. With each step towards the front door my anticipation rose.

The first thing I noticed about Brigid was how much she resembled her mother: delicate features and the same piercing eyes that revealed a quiet determination and perhaps a silent plea for answers.

'Please, come in.' Brigid's voice was a whisper, as if she was nervous to discuss the past.

We sat opposite each other at the dining table, and I took in the scene. Soft light filtered through curtains. I could sense Brigid was anxious: her fingers fidgeted, and she kept glancing at her partner, Jess. It was clear this conversation was not easy for her.

I leaned in, trying to give off a feeling of support and understanding. 'Brigid, thank you so much for letting me into your home today. I know discussing your mother is painful, but we just want to try to get to the bottom of what happened to your mum back in 2005. You were just 11 years old then.'

Brigid nodded, her voice barely audible. 'Yeah, I was only 11. Just a kid. I didn't understand much about what was happening. There were a lot of police involved after Mum was reported missing.'

I pressed on gently, hoping to unearth memories buried deep in the back of Brigid's mind. 'Do you remember coming up to Atherton back then? And the reason why you and your mother travelled up here?'

'Absolutely. We travelled up here on holidays because my brother, his partner at the time, was pregnant and my mum wanted to see the birth of her first grandchild. She was super ecstatic about it.'

Brigid remembered it being really hot, and living rough in tents on her mum's friend's property. She remembered her mum leaving during the day to go to visit friends, but she always came back. Until one day, she didn't.

'It must have been frightening for you. Were you and your mother often separated?' I asked.

Brigid shook her head. 'Not really. We were always, you know, next to each other. It was odd when she didn't come back.' Brigid's memories painted a picture of a carefree life disrupted by sudden, unexplained absence. 'I was told she was staying with a friend, but it didn't make sense. She was so excited about the baby, yet she missed the birth.'

I probed further, trying to understand the family dynamics at play. 'Did you notice anything strange between your mum and your brother?'

'There was definitely something strange going on. I don't know if my brother and mum were fighting but, as I said earlier, she didn't spend too much time in the camp. It was odd. The whole situation was strange.'

Her voice quavered as she recounted asking her brother Alan about their mother. 'He said she was visiting a friend and would be back in a few days. He said he dropped her off in Atherton on December 29, 2005 so she could play pool at the local pub. But she never returned.' Brigid shook her head, unable to make sense of it. 'It is definitely baffling as to why she wasn't there at the birth. It was the thing she wanted most in the world.'

So why would Katie miss the birth of her grandchild? After speaking to Brigid and her sister Lily, I became convinced that Katie had been a victim of foul play, that someone had harmed her and hidden her body so it had never been found.

It was an outcome no one wanted to imagine. Brigid tried not to go there. Talking about her mother's disappearance had been difficult but, like Lily, she wanted answers. She said her mum deserved that.

'She had such a beautiful personality. She loved everyone around her, cared about everyone. She was just a beautiful woman all through.'

I left Brigid determined to find out more. I'd arranged to visit the local police station, in the town of Mareeba, to speak to Detective Sergeant Brett Devine, who'd been handling Katie's case. I hoped he could shed some light on the investigation.

As I pulled into a carpark at the back of Mareeba Police Station, Brett Devine was waiting. He greeted me with a firm handshake. 'Hey, Meni, good to finally meet you. I'm in charge of Tablelands crime investigation branch. I took over Katie's case shortly after transferring here. It's a baffling disappearance with no credible leads.'

We moved into a vacant interview room, and I asked Brett about the importance of the first 24 hours after a disappearance. 'The first 24 hours are crucial,' Brett confirmed. 'You need to gather as much information as possible. Unfortunately, in Katie's case, it took too long to report her missing.'

Brett hadn't been involved in the police interview of Katie's son Alan, but he had meticulously reviewed it many times and still had questions.

To piece together Katie's last known movements, we drove to Atherton so Brett could show me where Alan said he'd dropped his mother off.

As he navigated familiar streets, Brett pointed out landmarks. 'Alan mentioned the hospital and a cafe on the corner. We're in Jack Street now, which matches his description.'

'Where did he leave her?' I asked Brett.

'Alan said that he picked his mother up in Ravenshoe and then drove her to a street in Atherton. And then she walked into town from there.'

Alan also told police that his mother intended to then make her way to a friend's house in Mareeba, more than 30 kilometres away. No one knows how she planned to get there.

Two weeks later, on 11 January, one of Katie's friends went to pick her up at the house in Mareeba but was told she'd never arrived. Two days after that, Alan went to the police to report her missing.

The Atherton Tablelands is a vast and wild area. As well as Mareeba and Atherton, it contains the town of Millaa Millaa, and as the investigation into Katie's disappearance progressed, police started to focus their attention on that town and on a second person of interest.

Francis Wark, a convicted rapist and killer, was living in Millaa Millaa in 2005. Wark is a sexual predator whose violence against women sends chills down the spine of even the most hardened detective. In late 2007, two years after Katie vanished, Wark brutally attacked a hitchhiker. He took her back to his farm, where he bashed, tortured and raped her for six hours. When Wark fell asleep, the woman broke free of the ropes he'd used to tie her to a bed and managed to escape.

In 2014, while Wark was in prison for the rape and assault, Brett Devine interviewed him about Katie's disappearance and that of another girl, 17-year-old Hayley Dodd, who had gone missing from Western Australia in 1999. Police had always thought Wark was a good fit for Hayley's disappearance and suspected murder, but it took them 22 years to finally convict him of the crime. Hayley's body has never been found, and she is still listed as a missing person.

The audio recording of Brett's interview with Wark has only ever been released to me. Brett played me the tape on his computer. 'This is the first time I ever spoke to him,' Brett said. 'I wanted to lay the groundwork for the WA guys but also touched on Katie's case.'

The tape crackled to life. 'The time is 9.04 am on Tuesday, March 25, 2014 at Lotus Glen Correctional Centre. Frank, do you know a lady called Kathleen O'Shea?' Brett asked.

Wark's voice was cold and detached. 'No, I don't know her.'

Brett pressed on. 'Kathleen O'Shea used to live in Millaa Millaa. She's been missing since early 2006.'

Wark remained evasive. 'I don't recall anyone by that name.'

Brett and I drove to Wark's farmhouse at Millaa Millaa. Given the horrors that had taken place there, the remote location felt eerie.

We parked the car and walked towards the locked gate. Through the trees and bushes that partly shielded the property from prying eyes, I could see the house. There was no one around – just the two of us and a pig grazing in the distance.

Brett reflected on the case. 'Wark's violent interstate history wasn't known here. His attack on the local hitchhiker revealed his violent past. With missing females in the Tablelands it raises suspicion.' Brett sighed in frustration, then continued. 'And of course, when he attacks the victim, then you learn that he's the major suspect in the disappearance of a young girl from WA. The first thing that comes to mind is: *What else have you done?*'

'What is your impression of Wark after spending time with him?' I asked.

'He's a unique individual, that's for certain. I guess he's what you would picture when you think of a psychopath. He's evil – cold and evil.'

Driving away, I thought about Lily and Brigid and their enduring pain. 'It's heartbreaking,' Brigid had said. 'You hope and wish they'll come back, but deep down, you know they probably won't.'

After Katie went missing, Brigid continued to stay with her older brother Alan for a few months, before Lily organised for her sister to return to live with her and other family members back in Melbourne. But eventually Brigid returned to the Tablelands, drawn by a need to be closer to her mum. 'It's surreal,' Brigid told me. 'It's like coming home to the last place Mum was. It's hard to explain, but it's comforting in a way.'

The police still view Wark and Alan O'Shea as persons of interest. Despite efforts, I was unable to contact either of them. I tried calling Alan when I was in Melbourne but without success. So I could only rely on the voices recorded during their police interviews years ago to get an idea of what they told police.

'The main challenge has been the lack of credible information from the last person to see Katie alive,' Brett said.

'He wasn't available to give evidence at the coronial inquest, and he was evasive with the initial investigating police. So that has been a stumbling block, and another person of interest is now serving a lengthy prison sentence in WA.'

* * *

Alan O'Shea has refused all police requests to be interviewed again about his mother's disappearance. He is not compelled to speak to police, and his reluctance may stem simply from his desire to move on from the past.

I left the Tablelands with more questions than answers but believing I had uncovered some startling connections and haunting revelations. I feel the police interviews and the vast openness of the rural landscape hold the key to the haunting mystery of Katie's disappearance.

The search for truth continues, as does the hope that one day Katie's family will find the resolution they so desperately need.

There is a $500,000 reward offered by the Queensland Government for information about Katie's disappearance and suspected murder.

11

Warren's Last Walk

Warren Meyer

The tranquil beauty of the Yarra Ranges National Park in the Central Highlands of Victoria is popular with locals and tourists alike. Situated between Melbourne and the Victorian Alps, the park's majestic views and hiking trails are magnets for anyone who enjoys the outdoors. Whether you're an experienced hiker or a novice bushwalker, the diverse landscape offers a variety of experiences to suit any level.

Warren Meyer was an experienced hiker who had conquered the Kokoda Trail and reached the Mount Everest Base Camp. He was fit, capable and always well prepared. During the Easter holidays of 2008, he and Zee, his wife of

Warren Meyer

31 years, were staying in Healesville, a picturesque town at the base of the Yarra Ranges. On Easter Sunday, Warren kissed Zee goodbye before setting off on what should have been a leisurely trek in the ranges. He promised to return in time for lunch in Healesville with friends.

The 57-year-old father of two was ever reliable, so when he failed to show, the peace of that Easter Sunday was shattered. By mid-afternoon the weight of anxiety became unbearable and Zee visited the police station to file a missing person report.

People don't just disappear into thin air. But in the case of Warren Meyer, that is exactly what happened.

Zee lives in Black Rock, a suburb nestled on Melbourne's Port Phillip Bay. In 2024, I arranged to speak to her at her home in an attempt to understand the circumstances around Warren's disappearance.

Black Rock is a modern trendy suburb with a shopping strip of high-end shops, cafes and restaurants. I drove through the commercial part of town and into streets of houses with manicured gardens, some surrounded by tall boundary walls. Arriving at Zee's house, I noticed she'd left the large remote gate open so I drove through and pulled up in front of the garage.

Before I had time to knock, Zee opened the front door and greeted me warmly. Once inside, I noticed brightly coloured artwork on the walls that I would later learn were Zee's creations, a distraction from the anguish of not knowing what happened to her husband.

Framed family photographs covered the top of a buffet, each a timeless memory. There was a photo of Warren that Zee told me was her favourite. 'This is the last photo of us together,' she said, her voice heavy with emotion. 'It was Easter Saturday 2008, and we were at the Healesville races. It was a beautiful sunny day.'

Warren and Zee had met while travelling, their shared passion for adventure making them a perfect match. 'I met Warren in Kathmandu,' Zee said. 'He was Canadian and I was Australian, and we travelled on the back of a converted army truck through 13 countries together to London, and fell in love bit by bit.'

On that fateful Easter Sunday, 23 March 2008, Warren had woken early to set off on the 10-kilometre hike. Zee remembered their last conversation vividly. 'He came over to the bed and I wished him a wonderful hike. I said, "I'll see you soon." He gave me a peck on the cheek and picked up my phone because it was fully charged, picked up his backpack and left.'

It was a simple, heartfelt farewell that still haunts Zee more than a decade later.

By lunchtime, there was no sign of Warren at the restaurant where they'd agreed to meet. Zee initially gave her husband the benefit of the doubt, thinking his trek had taken longer than expected or that he'd gone to shower back at their room. But as time passed she began to worry. *Has he been injured?* she wondered. *Perhaps he's unable to use his phone.*

'He's so reliable,' she told me as she recalled her growing concern that day. She tried ringing him, but the phone was dead. Zee sat at the restaurant table with her friends. 'The chair at the end of the table is sitting there empty [and] I just kept looking at it,' she said.

With Warren a no-show, Zee and some of her friends drove to the start of the trail and found his car still in the Dom Dom Saddle carpark. Sick with worry and fearing that Warren was injured, Zee filed a missing person report at the local police station. Police launched a search immediately.

Zee then faced the terrible task of informing her children, Renee and Julien, that their dad was lost. 'They both turned up, and we just held each other, trying to cope,' Zee recalled, her voice breaking. 'Jules went ashen, and Renee collapsed. It was paralysing.'

Reliving that awful moment still brought Zee to tears. Renee, Zee's daughter, who had joined us and was sitting beside her mother, grabbed Zee's hand and squeezed it tight. I found myself swallowing hard; it's difficult not to be affected when people show raw emotion.

Once everyone was composed again, I turned to Renee and asked her about her father.

'Dad and I were very close,' Renee said, her voice trembling. 'He was so intelligent, so logical and calm. I was in denial for days, thinking how could something bad happen to someone so lovely, and who I loved so much?'

Zee remembered that two young police officers took it upon themselves to stay and work overtime, driving around until 2.30 in the morning. But when they returned with no news, the family's feeling of dread deepened.

By 8 am the next day, a command centre had been set up, and dozens of vehicles and a food van had arrived. An intense air and ground search involving more than 150 police and volunteers was soon underway. Mobile phone tower records showed that Warren's phone had pinged from a tower about two hours' walk from the trail head. This meant that his phone had been switched on and was scanning for a signal at that point. The weather was perfect for searching, but despite the ideal conditions, no trace of Warren or the backpack he had been carrying was found. After five agonising days, the search was called off.

For Zee and her children it was a devastating blow, but they refused to give up the search for Warren. Every weekend that followed they returned to the bush, trudging through difficult, perilous terrain, hoping to find any clue to his disappearance.

'We searched for two years,' Zee said. 'The first year was weekly until the bushfires came. The Black Saturday bushfires halted things for a while, but we went back. The bush was gone and we could see everything.'

One day they found a small skeleton of an echidna on a piece of bark. Zee's hope was rekindled. 'If you can find a little creature like that, maybe, you know, something's there. Warren carried a bright yellow GPS, so I thought, *Wow, maybe we can find that!*'

From the beginning, authorities had assumed Warren's disappearance had been a case of misadventure, dismissing any thought of foul play. But Zee was adamant they were wrong. She believed something sinister had happened to Warren. In fact, she was convinced that her husband had been accidentally shot and killed by deer hunters in the area and his body disposed of.

'Yes, I believe that,' she said. 'Maybe they've destroyed the phone, maybe they've taken the backpack away and dumped it beyond where his body is. I think they've panicked. You see enough hit-and-runs to know that people will actually panic and get rid of the evidence.'

Zee's theory is based on the eyewitness account of a man named Craig McDermott, who was at his holiday home in the area that Easter weekend. The day before Warren went missing, Craig was startled by heavy gunfire between 8.20 am and 9 am. Craig, who grew up hunting, estimated there were between two and four shooters. 'Hundreds of shots, maybe 100 to 200,' Craig described in an interview with *60 Minutes*. 'High-powered deer rifles or something along those lines. Crazy shooting. It was just madness.'

According to Craig, he heard the sound of heavy gunfire on Saturday, the day before Warren went on his hike, and then again on the Sunday, the day when Warren disappeared. 'There was a good two and a half, three hours of constant shooting, and just mad shooting, shooting at anything.' When the shooting stopped, he went to investigate and found an abandoned campsite littered with empty beer cans and rubbish, proving there were people in the area.

Zee realised this was all just speculation, but her theory

about Warren being accidentally hit by a hunter's stray bullet made sense. 'You are not allowed to shoot in the area, you're close to homes and a major road, and Warren left early. People weren't expecting anyone to come through,' she said.

One former Victorian cop, Valentine Smith, has spent the last seven years trying to prove it. So from Zee's place I travelled across Melbourne to meet him. I wanted to see the area where Warren went missing and Valentine had agreed to take me there.

It was a cold and rainy day. When I turned up at Valentine's place he was well prepared, with maps, wet-weather gear, a GPS and plenty of water. I found him to be a confident man, well organised and meticulous. I bet he'd been a great boss back in his cop days. We loaded up the car and headed to Healesville.

With 40 years as an operational officer under his belt, Valentine knew first-hand the pain and suffering experienced by families of missing people. 'And it goes on until such time as the remains are found,' Valentine said. 'It's not just about knowing what happened. It's about bringing them home. We want a body.'

Over the years, Valentine had put plenty of time and energy into the case, tracking down new evidence and witnesses and compiling a detailed report for the coroner. He was certain that Warren's disappearance had been no hiking accident. 'As far as a missing person case is concerned,' Valentine said, 'I'd say it's heavily weighted towards human intervention, probably three to four times more likely than natural misadventure.'

I asked Valentine why he had been so quick to dismiss the police theory of misadventure.

'Okay, he's missing,' he said. 'Where's his equipment? His backpack, clothing, thermos flask? Nothing. And even if he walks off the tracks – and you'll see when you get into this country, it's not a walking track like 2 or 3 feet wide, it's 50 metres wide. If he left the track for any reason, his backpack should have been found. There was nothing.'

Valentine believed there were three probable scenarios, all involving human intervention. The first involved an escaped psychiatric patient, diagnosed as having homicidal thoughts, who had been found in the area where Warren was walking. However, there was only a 30-minute window where they could have crossed paths. Too little time to kill Warren and dispose of his body.

The next scenario concerned two illegal drug plantations discovered after Warren disappeared. In 2014 during Missing Persons Week, a caller to Crime Stoppers suggested that Warren had been murdered because he'd stumbled on a drug crop. The caller claimed that his body had then been buried using earth-moving equipment, and that it would never be found. In fact, Zee and the family had come across a small crop some distance from the walking track when they were out searching for Warren in the weeks after he went missing. This theory was discounted because of the distance of the crops from the track.

The most likely theory was the accidental shooting, meaning Warren walked into the line of someone's gunfire. 'There was a substantial amount of what was reported as out-of-control shooting,' Valentine confirmed, referring to the gunfire Craig McDermott had heard. 'From semi-automatic rifles coming from an area where Warren was expected to have walked into that morning.'

I wanted to recreate Warren's last known movements and hike the Monda Trail, as he'd intended to do when he set off that Easter weekend. It's close to where Craig McDermott said the shooting took place. Warren's body could still be in the forest somewhere, and if it was, then it was up to us to try to find him.

'If he was shot,' Valentine said, 'which I'm saying he probably was, then we should have found him. The fact we haven't would indicate that his body was interfered with after.'

But the old cop in me said that moving a body can transfer evidence, thus creating more crime scenes and potentially more problems for the crooks. If Warren was the victim of a shocking shooting accident, I wondered whether it might have been difficult to move his body far, given the terrain and lack of vehicle access.

To help with what appeared to be an insurmountable task, I contacted cadaver dog handler Julie Cowan and arranged for her to bring a dog to help us search for Warren's remains.

About an hour after leaving Valentine's house, he and I pulled up at the carpark where Warren had set off on his walk, never to return. There was a chill in the air, but it had nothing to do with the weather. I got out of the car and watched Valentine point to the spot where Warren had parked his car that fateful morning. *This case is like a complex jigsaw puzzle*, I thought. *I'm hoping I can put the pieces in the right places to form a picture that will tell us what happened to Warren.*

Julie Cowan and her expert cadaver dog team joined us soon after we arrived. Julie's dog Billie was a black labrador with a nose for the macabre. Previously she had found remains up to 40 years old, making her our best hope.

Julie had been here before: she had been part of the massive ground search that was launched for Warren when he was first reported missing.

We prepared ourselves for the trek ahead, packing water bottles, snacks and safety gear. I noticed that Chris and Mark from Julie's team carried steel prods. They explained they would use them to poke holes in the ground to release scents if Billie signalled an area of interest. They called it aerating.

We had to cross a busy road to reach the starting point of the track. Cars whizzed by dangerously close to us, causing me to push hard up against a guard rail. Valentine, who was walking in front of me, suddenly stopped, bent down and picked up something from the roadside. Turning to face me, he opened his hand to reveal a couple of gun cartridges. The discovery was both startling and ominous. Valentine speculated that someone had been hunting deer illegally, using night scopes to shoot from the roadside.

Pocketing the casings, we moved on. We had to find Warren, or at least what remained of him. His family were never going to give up, and neither would we.

We crossed the road and climbed over a small embankment to where the Monda Track stretched before us, a 5-metre-wide trail flanked by thick bush and towering trees. Valentine warned us of falling branches that could impale a person like a spear. He pointed to several sticking into the ground. I regretted not bringing a helmet. Valentine had estimated we would walk about 4 kilometres that day, into an area on the map that he had marked as a place of interest.

According to Valentine, the Monda Track was classified as grade 3 in difficulty, which meant it was suitable for people with some experience and average fitness levels. It would have been a piece of cake for someone like Warren Meyer, who, prior to disappearing, had been training to climb Mount Kilimanjaro in Tanzania.

The track was all uphill and steadily getting steeper. I'd expected a narrow walking track where I'd be buffeted by branches, but there was huge clearance on both sides – you could park a semi-trailer sideways and still have room. It was literally a walk in the park, even for someone like me who had never hiked before in his life.

But as I surveyed the dense wilderness beyond the trail, I imagined it would be easy for someone to get swallowed up within the rugged terrain. You could walk past or over a body and not notice.

As we neared the area Valentine had marked on the map, we reviewed the timeline using the Naismith Rule, a formula used by experienced hikers around the world to calculate distance and time. Valentine had calculated where Warren would have been when the shooting started. The timeline was tight, the clues tenuous, but it was all we had.

'It works on a principle of about 1 kilometre per 15 minutes, and then about an extra ten minutes per 100 metres' incline. So it puts us here, which is consistent with where the shooting was coming from,' Valentine explained.

We reached the top of the hill, a significant spot according to Valentine's calculations. It was about two hours from where Warren left his car, consistent with the timeframes and the location of the reported shooting.

Valentine had spent weeks up here with a metal detector, scouring the area for bullet casings but had found nothing. Yet he remained hopeful. 'It was also consistent with what the police determined was where the arc of the telephone ping of Warren's phone was recorded as coming from, and its close proximity to where a vehicle could be parked, which is just up here ten minutes.' Valentine pointed, suggesting it would not have been far for a couple of people to carry Warren's body and drive it out of the forest.

It was time for Billie the cadaver dog to get to work. Julie gave Billie a trigger word – 'Search!' – and instantly the little dog bounced off with energy and purpose. Her nose, a finely tuned instrument, hovered over every inch of ground as she swept a clearing in front of us, darting back and forth and side to side. Watching Billie work was mesmerising; she reminded me of a robotic vacuum cleaner programmed to cover every bit of ground. A GPS tracker on her collar ensured that Julie knew her location at all times.

We watched Billie disappear into the undergrowth, our hopes pinned on her extraordinary nose. To say the tension was palpable would be an understatement. After all, we were searching for human remains. Chris and Mark used their steel prods to aerate the ground, releasing any trapped scents that could guide Billie. The process was slow and methodical, each step a grim dance with the past.

'Good job. Good job,' Julie yelled as Billie showed some interest in a patch of ground near a creek that I could hear burbling faintly in behind thick, overgrown vegetation. The terrain was slippery from the rain, so following Billie, whose four legs were a significant advantage, was slow.

The sound of running water became louder as we approached. 'So, you want me to put her in this scrub here, into the water area?' Julie asked.

Billie the cadaver dog and Julie on the Monda Track

Valentine's response was a simple nod. Billie splashed into the creek, her lean body slicing through the cold water with purpose. Her ears pinned back, she reached the far bank, scrambling up with strong muddy paws and shaking off the water. She pressed her nose down to the ground, sweeping it back and forth in intense, meticulous movements. She traced the bank with a relentless focus, weaving over rocks and under low hanging branches, searching for even the faintest trace. Then she jumped back into the creek, her eyes fixed on the side we were standing on as she lunged forward. Reaching her starting point, she repeated the same careful routine with the same driven determination.

Her snout worked tirelessly.

We watched with bated breath as Billie searched. 'Find the backpack, or his water bottle, just the water bottle,' I said aloud. But after 40 minutes, Julie called her back. There was nothing there.

Disappointment settled over us as we turned and began the long trek back down the hill. No matter how big or difficult the task before me, whenever I investigate a missing person case, I do so with a firm belief that I will find something. A new piece of evidence, a new witness or, better still, the missing person themselves.

I walked ahead of the others, needing some time to myself. I felt like the air had been let out of me. As I surveyed the vastness of the area, I was overwhelmed. 'You could hide a hundred bodies here and no one would ever discover them,' I muttered to myself. My words seemed to hang in the air, a grim reminder of our daunting task.

We had hoped to find Warren that day, but our hopes had evaporated like the rain that had drenched the high country in the preceding days.

I thought of Zee and her children and felt I'd let them down. It reminded me of how much I hated the word 'failure'. It's a horrible word full of negative connotations. I'd wanted so much to find Warren's remains, but we hadn't.

Suddenly, a voice cut through my thoughts. It was Valentine, yelling my name and waving for me to come back up the hill to where he and the rest of the party were gathered. 'Billie's got something,' he shouted, his voice echoing through the forest. I turned back and raced to where the others were, my heart pounding with renewed anticipation.

When I got there, Billie was racing back and forth, her nose fixated on the base of a large tree. 'This is an area where we need to have a look,' Julie said excitedly. 'I'd like to probe the area in there because she's extremely interested. It's the only time that I've seen her show a heck of a lot of interest today.'

Chris and Mark moved in with their tools, probing the ground to release any scents that were trapped below. The steel rod slid into the earth, and we watched and waited in silence. Billie homed in on the same patch of ground at the base of the tree and lay down, her signal to Julie that she'd found something.

The area of interest was about ten steps off the track. Valentine took a large hunting knife from his backpack and began to cut through the thick vines and vegetation that covered the ground. When he reached dirt, he and Mark began to feverishly dig with their hands. We hadn't brought proper digging tools with us because we'd thought it was more likely that we'd find clothing or equipment that hadn't been buried. And if we did find Warren's body, chances were it wouldn't be buried very deep because killers are usually in a hurry to get the job done and get out of there.

The topsoil was a red-brown colour and soft. Each layer of soil removed could potentially uncover secrets buried long ago. Valentine and Mark dug about 20 centimetres down before striking the subsoil, which was harder to penetrate. It was a lighter colour and had a sticky texture, and without proper tools it was slow going. But they pressed on, driven by hope and desperation.

However, it soon became clear we would need to return with better equipment. For now, the search would have to be postponed. Valentine documented the area by taking photographs, both as a permanent record of our findings and to record the spot where we'd need to dig deeper when we came back.

We trekked back to our cars, with Billie's discovery and the promise of new leads lifting our spirits. 'I would love to dig deeper to see what can be found,' Valentine said with renewed enthusiasm. 'If there's something there, we should find it, you know, there was a very strong indication.'

I asked Valentine what he would say to anyone who had information about the disappearance of Warren Meyer. His response was terse and ominous. 'If you know what happened to Warren, you better speak up soon,' he said, his voice carrying a warning into the wilderness. 'Because things are about to change, and you better speak up, because if you don't, you're going to come unstuck very quickly in a big way.'

We left the Yarra Ranges and its secrets behind, and I rang Zee to tell her I was coming to update her on the day's events. She asked me to meet her on the promenade along

Port Phillip Bay, where she wanted to show me a special place she had created for Warren.

By the time I arrived, the sun was piercing the clouds and the bay glistened. The promenade was Zee's 'happy place' where she found solace. As we walked, she described seeing dolphins leaping out of the water and pelicans coming in to land like jet planes.

After Warren disappeared, she had wanted to keep his memory alive and to have a place where she could take her grandchildren and teach them about the grandfather they never met. We stopped at a bench. On it was a small plaque dedicated to Warren.

'The kids love it. They bring their little beach items and stick them in [the ground] around here. They're all hidden back there somewhere,' Zee said, 'and they told me one day that they're waiting for the night fairies to come and take them to Grandpa. Oh, oh, it tugs at your heartstrings that innocence.'

The bench was more than a memorial; it was a focus for Zee's grief and a place to reminisce. As she spoke of her walks along the sea wall, I sensed that her love and longing for Warren had never faded and never would. The bench was a testament to Zee's unwavering dedication to keeping his memory alive.

'I leave some flowers on those significant anniversaries, and so it's a focal point, and it's given me something because we don't have a grave. This won't stop with me passing. My children, you know, I really suffer for them because I know they've got decades of this. If we do not get answers, then of course my grandchildren … It won't stop.'

As we left the bench, the sea breeze carrying Zee's words, I couldn't shake the feeling that we were close. But being close wasn't good enough, because the Meyer family would still be left living in an emotional inferno where their grief was frozen in time forever, and there was only one thing that could change that.

'If I could find Warren, it would mean the world to us,' Zee said. 'It would mean we can bring him home with dignity. Even if there weren't many bones left, it would be something.'

* * *

Two weeks after we retraced Warren's walk on the Monda Trail, Zee and Valentine, together with a large group of their family and friends, returned with digging tools to excavate the site that Billie the cadaver dog had shown interest in. But despite working for hours and digging deep into the ground, they failed to find anything.

Valentine has vowed to return and try again. Zee has vowed to never give up on her quest to find Warren and bring him home.

Warren and Zee's daughter, Renee, believes someone holds the key to unlocking the mystery. 'Someone has answers,' she told me. 'I miss my dad so much, and not having answers makes everything more difficult and traumatising. We have no closure, and we need that.'

12

Loss of Innocence

Toni Cavanagh & Kay Docherty

In the middle of 2019, a group of old school friends gathered for a reunion, the 40-year anniversary of their departure from the halls of Lake Illawarra High School, south of Wollongong in New South Wales. The class of 1979 came together at the Warilla Bowling Club, and the once bright-eyed teenagers full of hope were now weathered adults, life's trials and tribulations etched on their faces.

Some of these classmates had remained close, their friendships enduring the test of time. Others hadn't seen each other in decades, the years creating a chasm that this night sought to bridge. Some had never left the old

Kay Docherty

Toni Cavanagh

neighbourhood, while others had travelled long distances to reconnect.

Though I was not one of them, I was there too, an observer with a purpose. I watched as they exchanged warm greetings, their laughter filling the courtyard of the club they'd hired. I watched them take out their phones as they shared photos of children and grandchildren. Old class photos were passed around and they laughed raucously at how young they once were. They pointed to the teenagers in the photos who didn't have a care in the world, evoking memories of a simpler time when life's biggest worry was passing a Maths test.

Yet, beneath the laughter, there was a heavy sadness, an invisible fog that settled over the room. Some dared to speak of it, but the mere mention caused voices to falter, heads to bow and throats to tighten with unshed tears. They tried to stay upbeat, particularly on a night like this, which was supposed to be about reconnecting and having fun. But it was difficult. They couldn't help but remember the horrible day in 1979 when their lives changed forever.

That year, two of their classmates, Toni Cavanagh, aged 16, and Kay Docherty, 15, disappeared without a trace. The girls had planned to go to the movies in Wollongong and were last seen on Shellharbour Road. After that, nothing. The case had haunted their classmates ever since.

Toni and Kay. Their names still conjured images frozen forever in time. Toni with her fair hair parted down the middle, and Kay with her ginger curls and freckles. They had just been kids settling into their teenage years, with futures full of life and promise. But that promise had been snatched away in an instant, leaving questions and heartbreak in its wake.

I grew up in Wollongong too, though I attended a different school. Even in those days before the internet, news of Toni and Kay's disappearance spread like wildfire. Their faces were on the front page of the local newspaper, the *Illawarra Mercury*, and their photos filled the nightly news. My friends and I were all around the same age as Toni and Kay, and their disappearance sent ripples of fear through our tight-knit school community. Many of my friends, especially the girls, admitted they were scared. Others, mainly boys, perhaps naively dismissed Toni and Kay as runaway teenagers seeking excitement. But as the days turned into weeks then months, it became painfully clear that something far more sinister was at play.

Kay's twin brother, Kevin, was among those at the reunion. When I'd learned about the gathering, I'd reached out to him, asking if I could attend to cover their story. At first, Kevin had been hesitant. He didn't want the night to become a morbid memorial to his sister and her friend. But after we spoke to the reunion organisers, they understood my intentions. I wasn't there to dredge up old pain for the sake of sensationalism. I was there to try to find answers, and to encourage anyone with information to come forward, to finally bring some peace to the missing girls' families.

The reunion wasn't just a bittersweet meeting for friends who had lost touch. It was a blatant reminder that, even after 40 years, the pain of losing Toni and Kay lingered.

Trish, one of the classmates, had known Kay since primary school. She recalled the bond they'd shared, how they got along well even as they drifted in and out of different groups through their teenage years. 'It's a long, long time ago,' Trish said. 'I can only imagine how it changed their families' lives. It changed mine. I wrapped my daughter in cottonwool, and she's still very rarely out of my sight because of it.'

Another friend, Sharon, said that, as the anniversary of the girls' disappearance approached every year, she couldn't help but wonder what might have been. 'I wonder if they would have got married? How many kids they would have had? They should be here tonight,' she said, her voice breaking. Sharon, who was particularly close to Kay, said her heart broke not just for her friend, but also for Kevin, for their parents, and for everyone left behind to carry the weight of their loss.

They say time heals all wounds, but I say whoever said that never had someone they cared about go missing. The disappearance of Toni and Kay changed the lives of everyone who knew them, and it changed them forever.

'Anything that's got to do with school, or anything that dates back 40 years ago, it's always in the back of your mind,' Kevin told me solemnly. 'It's something that we don't dwell on every day, otherwise it would probably rip us apart. But things like this bring it back.'

Kevin remembered that Kay wasn't even supposed to go out the night she vanished. She had wanted to go to her friend Toni's house and help her babysit Toni's younger sibling, but Kevin and Kay's mother, Jean, had been against it. But Kay had been insistent, and Kevin, trying to placate her, had offered to take her on his bike and to pick her up later. So their mum agreed to let her go.

The last time Kevin saw his sister, she was sitting on the handlebars of his bike, her laughter echoing down the road as the two of them climbed the hill to Toni's house. Kevin remembers Kay had to walk the last bit because he couldn't pedal up the crest of the hill. He made sure she got inside before he left for band practice.

A few hours later, as promised, he returned to pick her up. But when he knocked on the door, Kay wasn't there. Toni's stepmother told him the girls had gone to the movies.

Kevin didn't want to believe something was wrong. He rode his bike around for a while hoping they'd show up. But as the night stretched on, he knew he had to go home. 'It got to the stage where I thought, *I've got to tell Mum. What can I do?*' Kevin recalled. 'But at no stage did I think anything foul, anything wrong had happened.'

Kevin's mum's reaction was immediate and visceral. Desperate to find her daughter, Jean picked up the phone and began calling all of Kay's friends. But no one had seen Kay or Toni. A feeling of dread settled in Jean's gut; she knew with the certainty that only a mother could that something terrible had happened.

Later that night, they went to the police. Kevin remembered the long walk to the station and his mother's frantic voice as she tried to make the officers understand that this wasn't just a case of two girls sneaking out at night for some fun. 'They treated it as a runaway at the time,' Kevin remembered. 'And that's when the wheels fell off, I reckon, from the very start, once they treated it as a runaway.'

Back then, missing person cases weren't treated with the same urgency as they are today. I saw it first-hand when I was a cop at Kings Cross. So often, parents were turned away and told their kid would turn up soon. Kevin said that the police, assuming the girls had run away, told his parents to come back in 24 or 48 hours. It was a mistake that cost them precious time, time that might have made all the difference.

What later became clear was that, on the evening of 27 July 1979, Toni and Kay left the Cavanagh house around 7 pm, saying they were going to the movies. But their real plans were far more exciting. Friends of the two girls later told police that the girls planned to hitchhike into Wollongong, about 20 kilometres away, to go to an under-18s disco. They were last seen at the bus stop outside Warilla Grove Shopping Centre on Shellharbour Road around 7.30 pm.

'Everybody hitchhiked back then,' Trish explained to me at the reunion. 'Nobody asked for proof of age to go anywhere. It was pretty innocent, but it all changed that day.'

As Kevin and his parents waited, hoping against hope that Kay would walk through the door, Trish realised how close she had come to being in Kay and Toni's place. By her own admission, Trish was a bit of a rebel in her own quiet way. She often sneaked out of the house with her best friend, Toni, ready to take on the night with the carefree abandon that only youth can afford.

Just one week before the night that would change everything, they had gone out together, just like they always did. That night, Trish's sister had been supposed to pick them up but she'd forgotten. It didn't matter at first and they laughed it off and decided to walk home. But as the hours dragged on and the darkness deepened, what had started as an adventure turned into an ordeal. It took them nearly the whole night to get home, and by the time they finally stumbled in, Trish knew she was in trouble. Her parents grounded her, forbidding her to go to the disco the following week.

But rules had never stopped her before. When the next weekend rolled around, Trish jumped out of her bedroom window and sprinted to Toni's house. When I asked her about that night, Trish recalled it vividly: 'I was told that she'd already left, so I ran down to the main road, Shellharbour Road, where we used to hitchhike from, and they'd gone, so I just went back home.'

Trish didn't know it at the time, but missing Toni was a stroke of fate, a lucky twist that likely saved her life. 'It was probably a blessing that I wasn't with them,' she confessed to me, her voice heavy with a mixture of relief and guilt. 'But I also think that if I was there, there's safety in numbers. Would they still be here? That eats at me all the time ... I'm going to start crying.'

The question has haunted Trish ever since. What if? What if she had been there? Would things have turned out differently?

Kay and Toni weren't particularly close; they were part of a larger group. Kay was the more cautious of the two, everyone knew that. In fact, the two girls were polar opposites. Kay was quiet and studious, while Toni was loud and had a fun-loving nature.

I asked Trish if Kay would have hitchhiked.

'I'm not sure about Kay,' Trish said. 'Unless somebody stopped that they knew and that's how Kay got into the car.' But something or someone made her let her guard down that night, and then, just like that, the girls were gone.

As I made my way around the reunion, I was overwhelmed by the feeling that everyone's innocence had been shattered the day Kay and Toni disappeared.

'It made us much more aware of what was going on out there, and what *could* go on out there,' said Roslyn, another classmate, her voice tinged with a lingering sense of disbelief. 'We didn't think it would happen. There's no way anyone thought this could happen.'

Roslyn's grim reality-check was echoed by Sharon. 'A massive loss of innocence,' she said, shaking her head. 'We never thought anything like that could happen. You never worried about walking home on the streets at night. But after that, everything was different.'

A few days after the girls disappeared, their families received the first of two letters supposedly sent by the missing girls. The letters were postmarked from Darlinghurst in Sydney. In the letters, the girls claimed they'd gone away with friends and would be back soon. 'We got one I think seven days later. Then we got one two weeks after they disappeared,' Kevin remembered.

The letters seemed to confirm for the police that the girls had run away, but Kay's family felt something was off. 'The handwriting wasn't hers,' Kevin told me. 'There was a spelling mistake in it. They had forensic tests on the envelopes and letters. At first, they seemed to think the writing wasn't hers, then they tested it again, and they thought it was.'

Kevin believed his sister, an A-grade student, could have been forced to write the letters. He was sure she had made spelling mistakes on purpose, a secret cry for help. 'It was definitely under duress,' he said, his voice cracking with emotion. 'She was left-handed and wrote backhand too. It wasn't quite in backhand, but I spoke to Dad about it and I said they could have been forced to write these letters.'

Thirty years later, in 2009, a special police strike force reviewed the case and agreed with Kevin: the girls had been forced to write the letters, likely under the watchful eyes of their kidnappers. It was an attempt to mislead the police, to make them think the girls were runaways rather than victims of foul play. But just *when* the letters were written could not be determined.

Over the years, there were reported sightings of the girls up the east coast of Australia. Trish thought she had solved the mystery while on holiday. 'I and another friend of ours, Sybil, we'd gone to Queensland, and we both swore we'd seen Toni,' she recalled. 'We yelled out, and a girl turned around and looked at us. We ran after this poor woman, but it wasn't her.'

Something that I've discovered while covering missing person cases is a common cruelty for those left behind. You start to see your missing loved one everywhere – in crowds, on the street, in the faces of strangers. You get excited, your heart races, you shout their name, but when they turn around, it's never them. It's just your imagination playing tricks, a cruel reminder of the gaping hole they have left.

'It was a huge burden, especially on my mother,' Kevin told me. 'We lost Mum five years ago and she was pretty special. I was very close to her. Our whole lives revolved around my missing twin sister. Mum never gave up. Dad and his friends went to Kings Cross for weeks, just walking the streets, looking for her. It changed our whole lives.'

Kevin's parents died with broken hearts, unable to find peace. And Kevin, too, couldn't let go. He'd never stopped searching for his twin sister.

After his mother's death, Kevin made a decision that would tie him to his past forever: he bought the house they had lived in at the time of Kay's disappearance. 'There was definitely a reason behind that,' he admitted. 'Same reason I could have got married when I was younger, I could have had a family. I threw away a career. I didn't think of anything else at that time. I wanted to stay with Mum, and Mum didn't want to leave the house.'

The house held all their memories, the good and the bad. Kevin's mother left the porch light on for years after Kay disappeared, hoping her daughter would come home. Even after his mum died, Kevin couldn't let go of that hope. 'Mum never wanted to change the phone number for that simple reason, that Kay will call one day. And I suppose I've followed in Mum's footsteps. If she's out there, which I don't think she is, but the house is still there.'

Jean Docherty held on to the hope that one day her daughter would come home. Before she died, she made a plea on television, her voice trembling with emotion. 'If Kay's watching, I would like you to make contact because we still love you, and I still miss you, and I will always love you.'

Kevin said there was never a moment of surrender for his mum. As long as there was no body, no evidence to prove Kay was dead, Jean remained hopeful. And that's what's so merciless and bitter about having a missing loved one. Despite commonsense telling you they are no longer alive, you clutch tightly to the impossible dream. Perhaps it's that hope, no matter how much it diminishes over the years, that allows you to go on.

The tragic reality is that the chances of Kay and Toni still being alive are slim at best. The girls would never have put their families through such trauma. In 1996, detectives investigating the Ivan Milat backpacker murders visited the Docherty home. Milat, the notorious serial killer, had reportedly worked on a road gang in Kiama, south of where Kay and Toni went missing. While the circumstances of their disappearance bore similarities to those of Milat's other victims, particularly the fact that they might have hitchhiked, a connection to him could not be made. Milat died in October 2019 without confessing to anything.

In 2013, a coronial inquest into Kay and Toni's case was opened. Deputy State Coroner Geraldine Beattie ruled that Kay and Toni had been killed in an unknown location by an unknown person or persons.

There is a $100,000 reward on offer for information about the disappearance of Kay Docherty and Toni Cavanagh.

Paul Stevenson

13

The Last Ride

Paul Stevenson

Julie Stevenson has always had a gut feeling about what happened to her husband, Paul. It gnawed at her from the moment Paul, a keen motorcyclist, disappeared in Wonbah, a small town in Queensland. She has always believed that the locals knew more than they let on. That there was a feeling she couldn't shake, a sense that someone knew the truth but they weren't talking.

The discovery of Paul's motorbike should have been a breakthrough. It was found down an embankment, but that's where the trail went cold. Where was Paul?

Paul Stevenson, 47 years old, was the kind of man people called 'a good bloke'. A country boy at heart, he loved the bush and knew it well. There was nothing he enjoyed more than hopping on his prized Honda CB750 and tearing along the winding roads that cut through the deep valleys around Bundaberg.

A diesel mechanic by trade, Paul was heavily involved in his community. He was a man who lived for his family and his work. His wife, Julie, and their two children, Nikki and Tom, were everything to him. As president of the local junior rugby league club, Paul spent every weekend immersed in coaching, spectating and organising games and activities. When he wasn't down at the club he was at home or out enjoying the simple pleasures of life, such as camping, fishing and spending time with his family.

On 11 March 2012, this loving husband and devoted father got up early for what should have been a routine and leisurely motorbike ride. But that ride would be his last. He never came home. It was as if the earth had swallowed him whole.

At the time of his disappearance, the future was looking great and Paul had a lot to look forward to. His daughter, Nikki, was expecting her first child, and Paul was over the moon about becoming a grandfather, so much so that he fussed over Nikki, who was suffering from morning sickness. His son, Tom, was about to graduate from high school and start to forge his path in life. Paul appeared happy and content. So why would he vanish?

The disappearance of Paul Stevenson cast a long, dark shadow over Bundaberg, a town 400 kilometres north of Brisbane known for its famous Bundaberg Rum. Rumours swirled, accusations were hurled and suspicion permeated the air.

When Julie and I met in 2023, I could see the pain of the past decade etched on her face. She had just driven six hours from Blackwater to Bundaberg to speak to me and was still desperate to find answers. We met in the house she and Paul had shared, a home full of memories that was now rented out to a friend. Julie had held on to the house even after she moved away from Bundaberg, unable to let go of the life she and Paul had built together.

'He was a really loving husband,' Julie told me, her voice trembling. 'We did a lot as a family. He was so excited about becoming a grandfather. He loved his job, loved working. Everything was good. I just don't understand how he could be gone.'

On the morning of Sunday, 11 March 2012, Paul set out on a ride to Paradise Dam, a place he knew well. The ride would take him along the Gin Gin Mount Perry Road, a stretch of more than 100 kilometres that winds through lush green valleys and dense bushland.

I needed to see the area for myself, so Julie and I drove out of Bundaberg to travel the route Paul had taken the day he disappeared. 'This was the servo where he was last seen on the morning of the 11th,' Julie said as we passed a service station. 'The police showed us the CCTV footage. It was just his bike and he was coming out with his jacket. It was definitely him.'

We had an hour's drive ahead of us to get to the spot where police found Paul's abandoned motorbike. The road was nice and smooth, with long straight sections and gentle bends, the perfect ride for someone like Paul. We passed through Gin Gin, a town once voted Australia's friendliest, before veering south towards the town of Wonbah.

When Julie and I arrived at Wonbah, we got out of the car and crossed the road, where she pointed to a spot down a steep embankment that was overgrown with lantana.

'The helmet was sort of just down here a bit,' she said.

'So the helmet wasn't with the bike?' I asked.

'No, it was just up on the side of the road but out of view.'

I asked Julie when she had visited this place last, and I was stunned when she told me this was the first time she'd been back. She had driven past a few times over the years but had never stopped here.

'How does it feel to be back here?' I asked her.

'Oh, a bit surreal,' she said. 'I just sort of get that feeling that he's here somewhere, but, I mean, if there's a body here, it would be like dropping a needle in a haystack.'

When we crossed the road to return to the car, I noticed that Julie, who was behind me, had stopped and looked back. I wondered what she was thinking. She didn't have a grave site to visit her husband, just this lonely, isolated stretch of road where Paul might have taken his last breath.

'We've got nothing,' Julie said. 'Other people have a grave in a cemetery [where] they can go and talk to their loved ones. We've got nothing. All I can do is stand on the side of the road.'

According to Julie, Paul had got up sometime around 3 am. He was planning to go for a long ride and return in time for a 9 am meeting at the footy club. Julie expected him back home after lunch, but as the hours ticked by, her concern grew. 'We tried ringing his phone – no answer. It kept going to the message bank,' she said.

When Paul failed to return home that afternoon, Julie organised a group to go looking for him. It included her children, Tom and Nikki, Nikki's partner at the time and some of Paul's mates. Julie feared he had been in an accident and was lying in a ditch somewhere, unconscious. When Paul still hadn't returned or made contact by the next morning, Julie called the footy club to check if anyone had seen him. That's when she learned that Paul hadn't shown up for the meeting. 'And they hadn't let us know he didn't turn up for the meeting the day before,' Julie said, still clearly frustrated. 'So we went and got onto the police, and they said, "Come straight in."'

A massive air and ground search was launched to find Paul. Every available police officer from Bundaberg and the surrounding police districts was called in. State Emergency Services volunteers and members of the community – totalling more than 70 in number, many of them Paul's friends – scoured the area around Wonbah. The terrain was rugged and fraught with danger: sloping wet ground and thick vegetation. It was a huge task, but everyone pressed on, driven by the hope of finding Paul alive.

As the search stretched into the night, Julie's anxiety turned to fear. 'If there was an accident, they would have probably found Paul up in a tree or something, because he would have been a mess,' she said.

On 13 March, two days after the search had begun, a rescue chopper spotted Paul's motorbike down a steep embankment off the Gin Gin Mount Perry Road. The motorbike was lying on its side in a thick lantana bush. Paul's helmet was nearby, but he was nowhere to be found. His wallet, leather jacket, phone and sunglasses were all missing.

The discovery raised more questions than it answered. There was minimal damage to the bike – just a broken indicator and an ever-so-slight crack in the visor of his helmet, which puzzled investigators. Police examined the road near where they'd recovered the bike and could find no evidence of an accident. There were no skid marks, no broken glass, no blood.

Sergeant Rob Jorna, who coordinated the search, told me that a forensic crash expert determined that Paul's motorbike had not been involved in an accident. 'It appeared that the bike was placed there,' he said. 'There was no evidence to suggest a crash.'

Julie has always believed that the scene was staged. 'They pulled the motorbike out and it started first go,' she said. 'The key was in it.'

The search for Paul continued for days. Police checked dozens of mine shafts in the area but turned up nothing. They brought in a specialist cadaver dog from Brisbane to search a specific area, but still they came up empty. The police search was eventually called off, but Paul's family didn't stop looking. Julie told me they even hired a helicopter. 'My father swam every dam,' she said. 'He knocked on every door. He just kept going, and we walked so many hills, trying to find something, anything. But there was nothing.' In desperation, Julie sought the help of a clairvoyant.

In the days and weeks that followed, stories began to circulate around town. Some people said Paul had run off to start a new life; others suggested he had suicided. The police had to consider these possibilities and investigate every theory as if it were true. But Paul's family insisted that Paul would never have willingly left his family, especially with a grandchild on the way. It was unthinkable. 'Someone who wants to suicide isn't going to go and fuel up a motorbike,' Nikki told me. 'It just doesn't add up.'

Nikki was seven months pregnant when her dad went missing, and she's forever haunted by the knowledge that he wasn't around to walk her down the aisle when she later got married, and that he never got a chance to meet his grandchildren. 'I quite often say to my husband I would love to have known what Dad would be like with our kids,' Nikki said, her voice tinged with regret, 'but we never got to see Dad as a grandfather.'

***

One of the biggest twists in the case came two days after police recovered Paul's motorbike. Two local men contacted police to say they had seen a man fitting Paul's description walking on the side of the road not far from where the bike had been found. But their account was vague, and they didn't report it until five days after Paul went missing, which meant valuable time was lost.

Julie found this frustrating. 'Two men did say they saw him – well, someone that looked like him – walking down the range on Sunday, when they were coming home from golf. They didn't come forward until the Thursday, so it was a bit of a time lapse between when they saw him and when they came to the police.'

The men told police they didn't know that a search was in full swing for a missing man, a claim Julie found suspicious. 'They said they didn't realise Paul was missing, but there was a massive search underway. Everyone knew something was going on,' she said.

The two witnesses were interviewed by police, who took statements from them about what they saw. 'So, basically, they said that they saw someone who looked like a biker without a bike,' Sergeant Rob Jorna recalled. 'It was within the area the bike was located. It is possible that it was Paul Stevenson, but unfortunately the member of the public did not know Paul Stevenson and wasn't able to say it was him ... The description he provided matched Paul Stevenson, but we weren't able to confirm.'

It was a promising lead that unfortunately led nowhere. Some people questioned why the men didn't stop and offer the biker a ride, since he was walking, but it's easy to be critical after the fact. Perhaps the witnesses were in a hurry, or they didn't stop because the man they saw didn't wave them down. It's sliding-door moments like this that I find particularly frustrating with missing person cases. 'What if?' Two simple words. *What if* it had been Paul walking along the side of the road, and *what if* the men returning from golf had decided to stop? Would he still be missing?

In a bizarre twist to the case, one of these witnesses received a threatening phone call about 12 months after Paul went missing. I managed to track down the witness while I was in Bundaberg, and he agreed to speak to me over the phone on the condition that I didn't identify him. He told me that someone rang him and said, 'I know it was you,' then threatened the witness's life before hanging up. Police traced the call to a public phone box in the town of Rockhampton, 300 kilometres away.

The witness told me the phone call frightened him; he wished he had never seen the man on the side of the road or come forward. He went on to tell me that he believed he was being targeted by someone who blamed him for Paul Stevenson's disappearance. He reiterated what he had told the cops at the time: that he didn't know Paul and was unaware he had gone missing until a couple of days after passing the man on the side of the road. As soon as he found out police were looking for a missing man, he contacted them, something he now regretted because it raised suspicion about him and his friend.

I guess that's the thing with small country towns: loose lips are as common as beer and rodeos. Police have told me there is no evidence to link the two witnesses to Paul's disappearance.

***

Paul Stevenson's disappearance haunts the minds and hearts of those who loved him. The pain of not knowing, of wondering every day what happened to him, is unbearable for Julie, Nikki and Tom. And while I often talk about the emotional turmoil inflicted on families, there are other, rarely discussed consequences that impact loved ones left behind.

For Julie and many other families of missing people, the disappearance of their loved one can hit the family hard financially. Paul had been the family's main income earner, so when he disappeared it left a huge hole in the family's earnings, forcing Julie to make some tough decisions just to survive.

'It was difficult. I had the kids to look after. I still had a car to pay for, I had house payments, so financially it was really hard. Until they declared him deceased, I had to keep trying to make those payments for four or five years,' Julie explained.

'What happened to Paul's bike?' I asked her.

'I sold it,' she replied. 'My son didn't want it, so I sold it to pay bills. I sold a lot of stuff to pay for bills. My wedding rings, other jewellery I had to sell just to make the house payments and car payments. People don't understand that, apart from the emotional toll, he was the breadwinner and no one ever thinks of all these other things, how a family is affected economically when someone goes missing,' she said, dropping her head. 'My biggest regret was that I sold Paul's tools. He had thousands and thousands of dollars' worth of tools. I sold them, or more or less gave them away, just to get money to survive.'

In 2016 a coronial inquest found that Paul Stevenson is deceased, but just how he died is still unknown. Julie, however, believes she knows how her husband's life ended. 'Foul play is *my* answer,' she told me. 'I do believe that's what happened to him.'

The disappearance of this father of two continues to cast a shadow over the town of Bundaberg. His family remains resolute in their quest for answers. They believe that buried within the secrets and whispers of the town lies the truth, waiting to be unearthed.

Nikki told me her dad's disappearance makes no sense, and she will never stop looking for him, no matter how long it takes.

'There is no way in this world that someone can literally completely disappear,' she said. 'There is no way with no one not knowing anything. It just can't be possible.'

Rhianna Barreau

14

The Last Errand

Rhianna Barreau

Retired South Australian homicide detective Allen Arthur had an instinct, a nagging feeling, whenever he thought about the disappearance of 12-year-old Adelaide schoolgirl Rhianna Barreau. From the beginning, he'd known this wasn't just a case of a lost child. It was something darker.

His gut instinct told him that the answer to Rhianna's disappearance could be found within arm's reach of where the schoolgirl lived. Was it someone who also lived in her neighbourhood? Or was it a friend or someone who knew Rhianna? Whichever the case, it was clear that someone had seen an opportunity in a young girl who was alone, and they had seized it.

Police often encounter horrific crimes that give them a front-row seat to the worst and most depraved sides of humanity. They regularly deal with vile and awful people who really have no place in a civilised society. But it's those who commit crimes against children who we abhor the most, and who evoke in us the deepest feelings of disgust and moral outrage, because children are innocent and they cannot protect themselves.

That's why the disappearance 33 years ago of 12-year-old Rhianna Barreau really gets to me. I have a daughter around the same age, and the thought of her going missing terrifies me. I'm sure it's a fear most parents share.

Wednesday, 7 October 1992 began like any other in the quiet Adelaide suburb of Morphett Vale. The air was filled with the subtle scents of spring, and for Rhianna, who was on school holidays, it was to be a day filled with simple joys.

There was no internet or social media back then, and, like many kids growing up in the 1990s, she had a pen pal who lived in the USA. As Christmas was on the horizon, Rhianna, ever the thoughtful girl, had one thing on her mind: she needed to buy a Christmas card for her pen pal.

She wanted to send the card early enough to ensure it arrived before Christmas. It was a simple and kind gesture, an errand that would not take her long.

Rhianna's mother, Paula, kissed her goodbye and left to attend a course she was completing at a local TAFE, with plans to meet up again for lunch at the local shopping centre, the Colonnades. It was to be an ordinary mother-and-daughter outing, and one that would allow Rhianna to buy that special Christmas card.

Rhianna was planning to catch the bus to the shops, but in a twist of fate, the local bus drivers were on strike that day. However, the Reynella newsagency was a mere kilometre away, so the bright girl who loved listening to 'Love Shack' by the B52s decided to walk there and pick a card. The round trip would take no more than 30 minutes, and she could tick off the job on her to-do list.

I imagine she was happy that morning, her mind filled with thoughts of the holidays and her friend across the ocean. There was nothing risky in her outing. She left in broad daylight, in a safe neighbourhood, and intended to be gone for just a short time. But when her mother returned home that afternoon around 4 pm, the house at 47 Wakefield Avenue, Morphett Vale, was empty. The television was on, and the Christmas card Rhianna had been so desperate to buy was lying on the dining table, still in its paper bag from the newsagency. The only things missing were Rhianna's set of house keys and Rhianna herself.

Thinking her daughter might have gone to a friend's place, Paula called around to see if anyone had seen her, but no one had. Paula hadn't been concerned when Rhianna hadn't turned up for lunch – it was school holidays and there was a bus strike – but now she started to feel worried. She went door to door in the neighbourhood, asking if anyone had seen the 12-year-old, but Rhianna was nowhere to be found.

Panic set in, and at 6 pm that evening Paula went to the local police station, frantic with worry, and reported her daughter missing.

Within 48 hours, the young girl's disappearance had been declared a major crime. Veteran homicide squad detective Allen Arthur was put in charge of the investigation.

'My boss said, "There's a young girl missing and you better get down to her address. It doesn't sound good." So I jumped in the car with a colleague and immediately began an investigation,' Allen told me in 2023, his voice heavy with heartache.

Allen and I were sitting at the dining table in his house, nestled behind sand dunes on the south coast of Adelaide. Allen was 83 years old, but there was still fight in the old cop and a burning desire to see justice for Rhianna and her family after decades of not knowing what had happened to her.

For Allen, this case was more than just a file in the archives. It was a dark cloud that had followed him throughout his career and continued to cast a shadow over him. His eyes hinted at a deep sadness about a little girl he hadn't been able to bring home.

'Rhianna Barreau sticks in my mind,' he said, his voice quavering. 'I travel in the area where she was living, and I keep looking at the paddocks and thinking, *I wonder which paddock she might be in?* It's probably one of the most terrible investigations I was involved in, and unfortunately I wasn't able to solve it.'

In the first couple of days of the investigation, Allen had been able to construct a timeline of Rhianna's last known movements on the day she went missing, based on witness reports. At 10.30 am she left her home, likely heading to the Reynella Shopping Centre. Records showed she bought a card at the newsagency at 11.19 am. Later, around midday, she was seen taking a shortcut through the grounds of two local schools: Morphett Vale High and Stanvac Primary. Witnesses told police they saw her carrying a small bag, which was presumed to contain the Christmas card she'd just bought. That card was found on the dining room table in her home, proving she returned to her house. But what happened next is a mystery that only her abductor knows.

At the time, the city of Adelaide was grappling with devastating floods, stretching police and other emergency services, but Allen remembered that every available resource was mobilised to search for the 12-year-old. The investigation involved more than 70 police and volunteers, who combed through dumps, landfill and bushland for any trace of the young girl.

Among those on the ground searching was Rhianna's father, Leon, desperate to find his daughter yet weighed down by the terrible reality that she might be gone forever. He made an appeal during a local news interview, his words heavy with resignation. 'What I would really like is to have a policeman knock on our door and say that we will get her back in one piece, but the reality of that, I think as everybody knows, is fairly insignificant.'

Allen told me police searched backyards, parks and creeks and door-knocked the whole neighbourhood, interviewing anyone who might have seen or heard something. But there was no sign of Rhianna.

Every day without a breakthrough ripped into the souls of the missing girl's family. The lack of evidence just added an extra layer of anguish. In a city notorious for child abductions, the spectre of past unsolved missing children's cases loomed large: the Beaumont children in 1966, the Family Murders in the 1970s and 1980s, and the abduction of Joanne Ratcliffe and Kirste Gordon from Adelaide Oval in 1973.

News outlets carried Allen's public plea for help, together with his grim prediction that, without community help, the case would likely remain unsolved.

This thought plagued Allen's thoughts constantly. 'Without a result it haunts you,' he told me. 'It just aggravated me a great deal to think we hadn't come up with a solution, we hadn't managed to successfully bring the inquiry to a conclusion, be it by death or recovery.'

Allen's gut told him that they were unlikely to find Rhianna alive, but he remained determined to bring her home to her grieving family. He remembered questioning Paula Barreau about Rhianna's life, searching for any hint of trouble. Had she ever run away? Did she have a boyfriend? But nothing suggested Rhianna had willingly disappeared. Police searched her bedroom, looking for any clues, but it was neat and tidy. There were no notes or secret letters – nothing to suggest she planned to leave. It was as if she had stepped out the front door and disappeared into thin air.

Paula clung to the hope that her daughter might return, that it was all some terrible mistake. 'Please come forward,' Paula pleaded through tears on the nightly news. 'I just want my daughter back. It's not the same at home.' But as the days turned into weeks, that hope was sorely tested.

The streets where Rhianna was last seen were silent, and the small close-knit community where she lived was on edge, haunted by the unknown. The pressure on police was immense. They worked tirelessly to solve the case, following up more than 1600 tipoffs from the public, but none of the leads led them anywhere significant. They set up a mannequin at the shopping centre where Rhianna had been meant to meet her mum for lunch. It was dressed in the same clothes Rhianna had worn on the day she vanished. They even had Rhianna's friend, Danielle, dress as Rhianna and retrace the missing girl's last known steps. It must have been a heart-wrenching sight, watching this young girl who had just lost her best friend bravely walk the same path her friend had taken, hoping it would yield some clue.

Police also tried to track down a suspicious car that witnesses had reported seeing in the area, a white Holden Torana with Victorian number plates. Toranas were a popular mid-sized muscle car at the time. Police released details of the car to the public and were inundated with reported sightings. Allen told me they concentrated on trying to track down the car and its driver but, despite a nationwide search, neither the car nor its driver was ever found.

'We did everything we could,' Allen lamented. 'We were working 17 hours a day and it went on and on until we had to take a break. Every phone call we received we analysed, every comment was rehashed, just in case the person responsible was making a phone call [to throw the cops off the trail], but nothing came of it.'

Another tip came from a payphone, the caller reporting he had found a set of keys in a driveway matching the description of the keys Rhianna had with her when she went missing. But the witness claimed that by the time he returned to retrieve the keys they were gone. It seemed that every time police thought they were onto something, it ended in bitter disappointment.

The more Allen probed, the more he became convinced that Rhianna had been taken. 'Someone close,' he told me, his voice heavy with the weight of old memories. 'Someone living nearby.'

Allen believed that someone had been watching her, someone who saw an opportunity and acted upon it. 'She was on her own, walking her suburban street,' he surmised, 'and going by pictures of her at that age, she was an attractive young child, and without any doubt in my mind, someone saw that she was attractive and decided to take advantage.'

Allen's mind had wandered to a dark place. 'You know, a girl of her age would be trusting, and justifiably, most of the time, but then that individual turns up who double-crosses that trust, and she pays the price.'

Allen believed that Rhianna encountered someone with a twisted mind who would stop at nothing to satisfy their sick desires. Just thinking about what might have happened chilled him. 'They're just garbage people,' he said, shaking. 'The problem is they don't look any different from most people. They target their victim, and then they strike.'

I asked Allen how the case personally affected him, and he became emotional. 'Well, it's very personal. I feel like we've let the family down. It lives very unhappily in my mind and my police career.'

Many police can relate to Allen's frustration. As I've said

more than once, most cops have one particular case they were not able to solve that continues to torment them long after they've left the job. For me, it's the unsolved murder of a man named Billy Donnelly, who was found dead in Kings Cross in 1987. He'd been gagged and robbed. Despite the passage of time, Billy's case still plays on my mind, and I would love nothing more than to see it solved.

Cases like those of Rhianna Barreau and Billy Donnelly leave a mark on your soul that can only be erased when whoever is responsible is brought to justice and made to pay for their crime.

'Do you think there's a chance that Rhianna could still be alive?' I asked Allen.

'I don't think so, no, no, I'm sorry. I wish I could say she is, but it's very hard to keep someone locked away for more than 30 years. My feeling is that the person or persons responsible for her disappearance would have used her and then killed her.'

***

Thirty-three years ago, on a warm October day in 1992, Allen Arthur was given the difficult job of finding Rhianna Barreau. Despite his best efforts, he was unable to bring the little girl home to her family.

He is now nearing the end of his life, but he has one wish he wants to fulfill, one last critical investigation to solve. He must find out what happened to the bright-eyed girl who went shopping then disappeared without a trace.

He knows the chances are slim, but he holds on to the hope that someone, somewhere, knows something, perhaps a piece of information that has been kept secret for decades, or a memory that might unlock the truth.

Over the years relationships may have soured or twisted, loyalties may have unravelled, and it might now be time to do the right thing. Do you remember being told something by a partner or hearing a workmate or friend say something while drunk that has always stuck in the back of your mind as being odd or disturbing? It may seem like nothing, but it could be the missing piece of the puzzle that helps to solve Rhianna's disappearance.

Rhianna Barreau disappeared a long time ago, but the memory of the young girl still burns brightly in the hearts of her family and those who knew her. It's so long ago that there is every chance that whoever is responsible for snatching her is dead. But just in case they are alive and are reading this book, I have a message for them.

You may have got away with your heinous crime for more than 30 years, but don't think the police have given up on catching you. Rhianna's case is still an active investigation, and one day the authorities will knock on your door and haul your perverted self off to jail. I don't understand how someone so gutless and depraved can live with themselves. You're a coward, and I hope you have spent the past three decades constantly looking over your shoulder, and that you jump every time there's a knock on your front door.

There's a $1 million reward on offer for anyone who comes forward with information that leads to the conviction of the person or persons responsible for Rhianna Barreau's disappearance.

The sand in the hourglass counts down our days. Allen Arthur's hourglass is almost empty, but before the last grain of sand falls, he has this heartfelt plea.

'Pick the damn phone up. Ring major crime. I plead to people with information that might assist the police, to pick up the phone. Make the move, please, I beg you.'

Antoine Herran

15

The Missing Frenchie

Antoine Herran

The Gap at Watsons Bay is Sydney's most notorious suicide spot. There used to be an average of two deaths at The Gap each week, and over the Easter long weekend in 1998 police thought they had another one.

The sun had long since set, casting shadows across the notorious cliffs. It was a serene evening, deceptively calm, but something sinister was building.

'Did you see the person jump? I'm sorry I have to ask you this.' The dispatcher's voice crackled over the phone.

'Yeah, yeah,' came the shaken reply.

'Is it someone you know?'

'No.' The voice trembled.

'All right, we're on our way. Can you keep an eye out for the ambulance?'

'Okay.'

The tension was palpable, and the seasoned dispatcher had recognised immediately that this wasn't a false alarm.

'Did you see the person jump?' the dispatcher asked again, wanting to be sure of the facts.

'Yeah, yeah,' the caller replied.

'Can you see the body from where you are?'

'No, no, no.'

Soon the piercing wail of sirens could be heard as police and ambulance converged on the scene.

It's a mystery straight from the pages of an Agatha Christie novel, but set near the towering cliffs of Sydney's eastern suburbs. It involves a missing French tourist and a determined ex-detective who has spent more than 20 years trying to find out what really happened.

Michael Geronidis served 26 years in the NSW Police Force, retiring as a detective inspector. We'd met in 1984 when I began my police career at Darlinghurst Police Station, and we'd quickly become friends. We've remained mates ever since.

In April 1998, Mick was a young policeman attached to Rose Bay detectives. One day a file landed on his desk. It would turn out to be the most baffling case he ever investigated.

'There was a triple-0 call made from a phone box at Watsons Bay just below the stairs to The Gap,' Mick told me when I interviewed him about the case, 'and the person who made the call said that they had just seen a person jump from the left part of The Gap. So the police went up there. There was a backpack on the path with a torch illuminating the backpack saying, "Here I am, have a look." The backpack belonged to [Antoine] Herran. All his property was in there, including ID, but no passport, so they immediately called the helicopter out, assuming he had jumped off the cliff, because the person on the phone had said he'd seen someone jump.'

Antoine Herran was a Frenchman who had been holidaying in Australia for three weeks. He appeared to have deliberately left his backpack to be found, presumably so authorities would know who he was and therefore be able to track down his family to tell them the tragic news that he had jumped to his death.

Police launched a large search to find Antoine's body in the crashing waves and jagged rocks below The Gap. Mick said it didn't take long to find something. 'So the next morning they found two bodies down there. There was a female who jumped off down towards the park, and there was another fella who jumped off.'

The bodies were retrieved and taken to the morgue for identification. Believing the male body to be Antoine, NSW Police contacted his parents and sister in France to break the devastating news that their son and brother was dead. 'I felt very sorry for the parents. They were shattered. They were very, very upset,' Mick recalled.

After landing in Sydney, Antoine's parents and his sister, Sophie, were met by police, who took them straight to the morgue to formally identify Antoine. But when they pulled the sheet back to reveal the dead man's face, everyone was left reeling.

'It was the wrong person,' Mick said. 'That was a big shock to them. And then to find out that he was missing and no one knew where he was – that was an extra shock.'

The male body recovered from the water was later identified as an escaped psychiatric patient. So where was Antoine?

Mick questioned Antoine's parents, probing them for any information about his life or any personal problems he might have been experiencing. But Antoine's dad and mum insisted there was no obvious reason for Antoine to take his life. 'He was very happy to come to Australia because it was his favourite place, and he would often say he would like to live here,' Mick remembered Antoine's parents telling him.

Baffled by this bizarre turn of events, Mick listened again to the haunting triple-0 call and his suspicions were aroused. 'The guy who made the call from the phone box at The Gap had a very strong French accent, and that was an indicator straight away.' Mick played the call to Antoine's parents, who identified the voice as their son's.

While pleased that the news could mean their son was alive, Antoine's parents were puzzled by the fact he'd made a prank call. 'We have lost our son,' Jean Francois said tearfully in an interview with *Today Tonight* a week after Antoine disappeared. 'We think that he had seen something that he ought not to have seen and something happened, but why was he there at that time?'

There was no evidence to support this theory, however.

To try to find out why Antoine was at The Gap and why he'd called triple-0 pretending to see someone jump, Mick painstakingly retraced Antoine's last known movements. 'He was due to leave for France that day, so he'd been out to the airport and checked in and checked his bags in. He asked if he could have a middle seat because I think he thought that if he had a middle seat no one would notice he wasn't on the plane,' Mick told me. 'He then went into the city, where he caught a ferry from Circular Quay to Watsons Bay.'

Then that night, at 2 am on Easter Sunday, Antoine used a public phone box to report his own death.

Mick was convinced it was all an elaborate hoax. He pointed to not only the phone call but also the backpack containing Antoine's identification documents and the torch that had been positioned to shine on it so it would be found. Everything had been staged to make it look like he'd taken his life.

But why go to all that trouble? Mick believed the answer to that question was simple. 'He liked Australia. He'd had a very nice trip. He was in Far North Queensland, he went to the Northern Territory where he went on helicopter trips. He even made an inquiry while he was here on how he could get to stay in Australia, but he was told, "You can forget it, you'll have to go back." So I believe he then started to devise a plan to make himself disappear.'

During his investigation, Mick tracked down the immigration lawyer Antoine had consulted about getting residency. 'He told him he'd have to go back and try and do it from France and get all the paperwork right,' Mick explained, 'but he wasn't happy with that.'

So Antoine devised a plan he thought was foolproof to go undetected and remain in the country. 'He figured out a good way to stay and probably thought no one would worry too much about it,' Mick said. 'He's caused his family untold pain and suffering but he's still here.'

Over the years I've wondered what Antoine has been doing and where he's been living. I've also thought about his poor family and the struggles they've faced not knowing whether he's alive or dead. Social media was non-existent back in 1998, and the internet was still in its infancy. Determined to find answers, in 2024 I began searching for his sister, Sophie.

It was a long shot, because if Sophie had married, she may have adopted her husband's surname, and how would I find her then? I searched French Facebook but came up empty. I then discovered a website called Copains D'Avant, 'Old Friends', designed to connect French people who were looking for long-lost contacts. To my surprise, I found Sophie listed, but there were no contact details for her. But the place where she worked as an Italian teacher was listed, so I sent an email to the school.

Within hours a very excited Sophie emailed me back. We arranged a day and time to speak, and a couple of days later I rang her from Australia. Early in our conversation it became apparent that time had not healed the wounds inflicted by Antoine's disappearance. He's never contacted them to let them know he was alive.

'I am … Well, it is very difficult for me,' she began in halting English. 'I am an Italian teacher, my English is not so good,' she apologised, 'but to think of my brother is difficult.'

Her voice wavered as she continued. 'My parents only want to know he's alive and in good health. We don't need to know where he is, just that he is safe. When someone goes missing and you have no answers, it's difficult to live every day.' Sophie said the tyranny of distance had made it even harder for her family to cope. 'Every day you think of him, and you can't do anything because it's in Australia, not in our country. It's the worst because we can do nothing.'

Sophie vividly remembered the day they received the call from the other side of the world. 'I was in Venice with my mother for a holiday. My father was away for work. My brother was supposed to return on a Sunday at seven o'clock. My mother felt something was wrong. Hours passed, and

Antoine didn't call. My ex-husband went to our house to check, but there was nothing, no luggage, no sign of him.'

While there was no indication that Antoine had returned home, Sophie's husband noticed a light flashing on the answering machine. Someone had rung and left a message. He listened to the message and wrote down the caller's number then rang Sophie.

'I called the number, but I was in Italy, and it was difficult to speak and understand English,' Sophie said. 'The girl said to me, "He takes his own life." For me, when I translated, it meant he take his luggage and goes away. Never did I think it meant he committed suicide.'

The terrible news of her brother's death was lost in translation. 'Someone from Australia tells you your brother has taken his own life, meaning he committed suicide, but I did not understand.'

Sophie pleaded with the caller to explain. 'I'm sorry, I don't understand. Can you tell me again?'

The policewoman on the other end of the line went and found someone who spoke French, and a kind voice finally broke the tragic news. 'Your brother has taken his own life.'

'We returned to France and my father called to our house for Antoine. I answered and he said, "Why are you at home,

Sophie, and not in Italy?"' Sophie's voice was breaking as she remembered that phone call. 'I say to him, "Papa, you must return immediately!" Imagine, he is in Brittany, it's three or four hours away in a car. Imagine, during the drive, wondering what happened. But he raced home to find no Antoine. I think it must have been so hard and terrible for him.'

Sophie and her parents didn't even have time for the awful news to sink in. They booked the first flight to Australia. NSW Police met them at the airport and took them straight to the morgue.

'We go to Australia to see the body, and it wasn't him. I remember exactly the moment when the police showed us and I saw the body of this dead man, and it wasn't my brother. It was terrible. All these thoughts raced through my brain: *He's alive! He's not alive.* After three days, we returned to our country with nothing.'

Back in France, the family contacted local authorities for help, but the French police were indifferent. 'It's good if he's alive. He's an adult and he can do anything he wants,' they said dismissively.

Life changed irrevocably for Sophie Herran when her brother, Antoine, disappeared. The weight of suddenly being the only child was immense. 'For my parents, he was a child, the only other person in our family,' Sophie recalled. 'For two years, I didn't know how to move, how to speak with my parents. Every time we mentioned Antoine, we started to cry. We couldn't help it.'

Over the years, Sophie tried to navigate the implications of her brother's actions. She made decisions that she now questions. 'I chose to marry two years after he disappeared. It was a mistake; now I'm divorced. He was my only brother. Our parents gave us so much love and opportunities. I don't understand why he did this. It forced me to stay in Normandy, to be with my parents in case my brother returns. It changed our lives completely.'

Families of missing people make decisions that take into account a whole lot of what-ifs around their missing loved one. 'I would have liked to do other things but because of him everything changed' Sophie explained. 'Our lives changed. It's easy to say that we make our own choice, but it forced me to do something else.'

Antoine's car became a symbol of her brother's absence. 'I used his car for two years, and every time I drove it, I thought, *This is my brother's car, but my brother is not here.* Every day was very, very difficult.'

When Sophie reflected on the months before her brother vanished, she realised there were signs that something was amiss with her younger sibling. 'He lost his job and was very angry at Christmas. It was terrible because he didn't offer a gift for the first time in our lives, and my parents were very sad.'

It wasn't only Christmas that haunted Sophie. Other anniversaries trigger more sadness. 'He took the plane to Australia on my birthday, March 17, the last time I saw him. That is horrible for me. These things are hard to forget.'

It's not a crime to go missing, but the pain and suffering inflicted on the loved ones left behind are a different story. 'Sophie, are you angry with Antoine?' I asked.

'Yes, yes, I am angry with him,' she admitted. 'When we came to Australia my parents made a video for television. I didn't want to do it because I was too angry, and now, I am still angry. It's horrible for my parents. I only want to take him in my arms and say, "Even if you did these things, I love you. I love you."'

Sophie said she had a recurring dream. 'For me, I'm sure he's alive. I don't know why but I feel him every day. I am at the ticket office to take the boat in Sydney, Australia, and I feel something behind me. I turn around and I recognise him immediately. He's with a woman with long blonde hair and two children. I say, "Hey, Antoine," and they disappear. I feel in my body that he's alive.'

'If your brother is alive,' I asked her, 'what type of work do you think he would do in Australia to survive?'

'Any work he can do. Perhaps in a restaurant or a hotel because of his French language, but if he wanted to disappear, he might not use French. He also speaks Italian and German, so maybe something involving work with tourists. He worked in logistics back home, so he's capable of many things. Now, 26 years later, he probably speaks like an Australian, without his French accent. Who knows?'

While Antoine has managed to stay under the radar for many years, Sophie isn't giving up and neither are Mick and I. Antoine has the right to begin a new life and sever contact with his family, and we would never divulge his whereabouts if he didn't wish us to do so. It's important to note that police respect a missing person's desire to stay undetected. All that anyone would do is let Antoine's family know that he's alive, so that they can try to move on with their lives.

'Will you ever stop looking for your brother?' I asked Sophie.

'No, no,' she replied firmly. 'I wanted to go to Australia to do my own search, even though I didn't know how. But I'm very happy you and Michael Geronidis continue to do this job. I've tried writing to Antoine on the internet, and searching police reports,' she said, sounding exhausted.

'What would you say to Antoine if you could talk to him now?'

'I love you, and I hope you are fine, that you are good and are happy in your life. More than 20 years ago you made a choice. I can accept your choice, but you must tell us you are alive because we need to know. For us, for our parents, you must tell us. It's too difficult to live like this. Every day I think of you. Everything reminds me of you.'

Sophie is now almost 50 and her parents are in their late 70s. Every day for them has been a struggle filled with pain and unanswered questions. 'My parents must not suffer another misfortune. Antoine must think of us. We are his family. We love him. We only want to know he is alive and well.'

There is no evidence that Antoine Herran is deceased. Sophie thinks he may be living in Far North Queensland or Tasmania, places he once said were his favourites.

Sometimes truth is stranger than fiction. Antoine has vanished, not into the water below The Gap but into a new life, somewhere in Australia, probably hiding in plain sight. The meticulous planning, the emotional turmoil inflicted on his family all point to a man desperate to escape his past and forge a new identity and life.

The search for Antoine will continue, driven by the unwavering love and hope of his sister and parents.

Antoine Herran would be 55 years old today. He is 182 centimetres tall, of medium build, with brown hair and blue eyes. He wears very thick prescription glasses. On his abdomen, he has a scar in the shape of a question mark.

Afterword

The stories in this book paint a haunting portrait of families clinging to threads of hope, even as the weight of uncertainty about their missing loved one grows heavier. But it's not just about loss. It is also about the fierce and undying need for truth. This book honours the tenacity of those who refuse to give up, who refuse to let go, who believe, no matter how much time passes, that someone, somewhere, knows something.

I cover every story with an unyielding commitment to find those who are missing and to return them to their families, or at least give their families answers. There have been breakthroughs in some cases, taking us a step closer to uncovering the truth, but there have also been disappointments – those moments when a promising lead comes to nothing, and families are left to start all over again.

Law enforcement, too, does not forget. Though cases may grow cold, they are never abandoned. A single new lead, just one fragment of information, can reignite an investigation, sending detectives back down long-forgotten paths, chasing the possibility of long-awaited answers.

This relentless pursuit of truth was evident once again in 2025, in relation to one of the world's most haunting mysteries: the disappearance of the Beaumont children. On 26 January 1966, the three siblings – nine-year-old Jane, seven-year-old Arnna and four-year-old Grant – vanished from Glenelg Beach in Adelaide, their fates a question that has tormented a nation for decades. Yet, even after all these years, their names still command headlines.

In March 2025, a glimmer of hope emerged. An extensive excavation at an old factory site in Adelaide's west promised the possibility of resolution, perhaps even the discovery of their remains. For seven days, thousands of tonnes of earth were turned over, each shovelful carrying the weight of expectation. But as the final day of the dig arrived, so too did disappointment. The search ended with nothing. No answers. No justice. No peace.

For the families of the missing, the search never truly ends. It becomes an inseparable part of their existence, as natural and necessary as drawing breath. Hope flickers – sometimes faintly, sometimes fiercely – but it never dies.

My team and I will continue to look at the probable and the possible, and to probe and prod consciences and memories with steely determination, because clearly someone, somewhere, *does* know something.

Acknowledgements

First and foremost, I want to thank the families of the missing. Your strength, honesty and courage in sharing your stories with me is something I will never take for granted. Your trust and honesty in the face of unimaginable grief made this book possible. I'm deeply grateful for the chance to help tell your loved one's stories.

To the police officers who gave their time and insights, thank you for your continued commitment to these cases.

Thank you to the team at HarperCollins for their support during the publishing process. Mary Rennie, Madeleine James, Jude McGee and Emma Dowden, I appreciate your involvement and assistance in helping bring this book to print.

To those who are missing: this book is for you. You are not forgotten. Someone, somewhere, knows something, and we will keep searching.